The Minimalist Griller Handbook

by

Oliver Abel IV

DORRANCE PUBLISHING CO., INC.
PITTSBURGH, PENNSYLVANIA 15222

ISBN # 0-8059-4523-7
Printed in the United States of America

First Printing

For information or to order additional books, please write:
Dorrance Publishing Co., Inc.
643 Smithfield Street
Pittsburgh, Pennsylvania 15222
U.S.A.

Dedication

I dedicate this book to the memory of my father, Oliver Abel III, who through untiring example encouraged me to embrace the simple things in life.

Table of Contents

Acknowledgements

I would like to thank my loving wife, Robin, and my two children, Jennifer and Oliver, for their inspiration, guidance, and unfailing cheerfulness in the wake of sampling, week after week, the grilled and smoked precursors to the recipes found in this book.

I would also like to thank my close friends, Pat and Susan, for their encouragement, enthusiastic editing, and much-needed textual suggestions.

Finally, I would like to thank my mother, Peggy Abel, for her many recipes that made their way into this handbook and inspired other recipes and cooking techniques true to minimalist grilling.

Introduction

For a large party, a few close friends, or just an intimate dinner for two, grilled food should be fun to prepare and fun to eat. If not, why bother? Sadly, many people don't bother, or they don't venture beyond the ubiquitous hamburgers and hot dogs found at most Memorial Day and Fourth of July cookouts. For far too many people, grilling is simply a chore.

To have a grilling party become a successful adventure, the first requirement—fun to prepare—simply takes a good selection of easy to follow recipes. These recipes don't require costly exotic ingredients or lengthy preparation time, and do use easy-to-understand grilling techniques.

The second requirement—fun to eat—happens only if your guests become involved in the whole grilling process: from lighting the charcoal to grilling the food to sitting down and enjoying the much anticipated meal.

Traditional grilling techniques and recipes usually cannot satisfy these two important requirements. All too often I've struggled to console well-intended, would-be grillers whose laments include:

- "I wouldn't know where to begin, much less how to use the equipment—even if I knew what equipment to buy, which I don't!"
- "It's just too complicated and I would cremate whatever I put on the grill!"

- "It takes too long to start the fire, so why bother?"
- "I have tried, but my gas grill doesn't make the food taste great, so I have given up."
- "The recipes I have seen appear to be written only for chefs trained at the Culinary Institute of America!"
- "The recipes require ingredients that you must pick fresh from gardens in Southern France!"
- "There are too many recipes from which to choose. How do I know which ones will taste good and which ones will complement one another?"

It is easy to understand the frustration of these would-be grillers. The anxiety associated with preparing the meal, the time involved with assembling the vast array of ingredients, and the uncertainty over how the unfamiliar recipe will taste are the bane of many a griller. Just look at the ingredients for the following traditional recipes taken from two popular grilling cookbooks; it is easy to understand how they can convert even the most enthusiastic griller into a frequent patron of catering establishments.

Hickory-Smoked Trout

- trout
- chopped onion
- butter
- dried apricots
- orange juice
- sugar
- instant chicken bouillon granules
- celery salt
- dry bread cubes

- toasted slivered almonds
- cooking oil
- hickory chips

Doctored Hamburgers

- ground beef
- pork sausage
- egg
- water
- dry bread crumbs
- oregano
- fennel seed
- garlic salt
- onion salt
- pepper
- hamburger buns

When I see traditional recipes like the previous two, it becomes immediately clear why grilling is not a more popular backyard phenomenon. First, the ambitious host ponders the different ingredients that must be bought, where to buy them, and the cost of each. He then turns his attention to the proper grilling or smoking techniques that might be best-suited to the meal. Then, after considering all the ingredients, preparation time, and grilling effort that will go into the meal, the host begins to wonder whether the guests really will taste the separate ingredients, much less appreciate the time and devotion that must be dedicated to the meal. Finally, and without any further thought or regret, the host quickly recovers his senses and surrenders to the appeal of the easy to grill hamburger and hot dog.

This handbook is written for the "as yet unskilled" backyard chef who is looking for an alternative method to traditional grilling that will put the fun back into grilling for family and friends. This alternative method, the minimalist approach to grilling, is different from traditional grilling in two respects:

- It celebrates elegance in simplicity—Never draw attention away from the natural taste and textures of the food; and, more importantly, never draw attention away from family and guests with needless preparation and grilling.
- It is a method that has been refined neither by a chef nor someone formally trained in the latest culinary techniques, but someone self-taught with the aim of creating simple, great-tasting, and elegant grilled meals for family and friends.

To convince the backyard chef to grill more than just occasionally requires meals that are as enjoyable to prepare as they are to eat. Because so many of my friends have said to me: "You make grilling look so easy!"; "You are a male Martha Stewart!"; "How did you think of cooking such a unique meal?"; "Can I be your sous-chef?"; and last but not least, "How do I get started, I don't even own a grill?" I have decided to put on paper my grilling philosophy, techniques, and favorite recipes. Hopefully, my minimalist approach will make grilling more enjoyable so that delicious, elegant grilled meals become more the norm.

All of the accompanying recipes in this handbook use few ingredients, most of which can be found in the average kitchen. Those that are not found in your kitchen pantry shelves can be easily purchased at your local supermarket.

Excluding the fresh meat, fish, vegetables, herbs, fruits, and dairy products, as well as the rice, pasta, breads, chips, and beverages (both alcoholic and non-alcoholic) that you need to purchase before any backyard get-together, the following is a list of every ingredient that you will need for preparing *all the recipes in this handbook:*

I. **Herbs and Spices** (most likely found in home pantry)

- dried tarragon
- dried onion
- dried parsley
- dried rosemary
- dried ginger
- cinnamon
- nutmeg

II. **Staples** (most likely found in home pantry)

- salt - regular and coarse (kosher)
- pepper - whole peppercorns in a mill
- vinegar - regular balsamic, white balsamic, and red wine
- oil - olive, and sesame
- ketchup
- mustard - prepared and Dijon
- sugar - granulated and brown
- Worcestershire sauce - regular and white wine
- soy sauce (light sodium)
- cooking sherry
- canned chicken broth
- peanut butter
- maple syrup
- mayonnaise
- liquid hot pepper sauce
- flour
- yeast

III. **May Need to be Purchased**

- bottled salsa (optional)
- bottled cocktail sauce
- pizza sauce
- marinara sauce

- crushed garlic (in oil), so you need not buy fresh garlic
- lime juice
- lemon juice
- tomato juice
- orange juice
- canned cooked beans
- frozen lemonade
- cornmeal
- marshmallows

In contrast to traditional grilling, minimalist grilling requires only a few necessary ingredients and as little grill time as possible. All of the appetizer, vegetable, and dessert recipes in this handbook require less than thirty minutes of grill time, with the exception of one (which requires thirty to forty minutes, due to the use of wood chips). Quite frankly, I cannot endorse spending much more grill time on these three courses—it is simply not needed. With respect to the recipes for the entrees, most also have grill times under thirty minutes. The few entree recipes that take more than thirty minutes have been included because the taste and presentation are so unusual and satisfying that they are worth the extra time. Only three recipes have a grill time in excess of ninety minutes—smoked turkey, pork roast and pulled pork sandwiches (and for good reason, as you will see).

Unless you grew up on a steady diet of steaks, ribs, and other high cholesterol red meats grilled by your dad, you probably don't know where to begin your grilling culinary education. Consult one of the many barbecue books currently on the market and you will be deluged with information about every type of grill (gas, kettle, and hibachi); every source of heat and fire (propane, charcoal, wood, electric—which, when turned on, will cause a brown-out in your immediate neighborhood); every kind of charcoal starter (lighter fluid, electric, self-starting, chimney); and the usual way of determining the temperature of the fire—(if you hold your hand over the fire for five seconds and develop third-degree burns, then it is ready for grilling). The grilling *process* can also seem overwhelming: direct and indirect fires, air vents, when to use the grill-top, knowing when the food is properly grilled, and when to use wood chips to create a smoky taste. As far as I am concerned these books provide too much information, much of it not easily understood by untrained chefs, and therefore the likelihood of any grilled meals in the foreseeable future is not very great.

This minimalist handbook will demystify the accessories and the grilling process. It will help you to select the preferred grill type, the method for starting the preferred heat source, when to use the grill-top or lid, and when to wood smoke the food (including which wood to use). It will also list which ingredients to use (never using more than absolutely necessary), and how long to leave the food on the grill. This handbook will also provide you with over seventy-five minimalist recipes to accompany your minimalist grilling and smoking techniques. In addition, you will find fifteen of my favorite grilled meals (including an appetizer, entree, vegetable/side dish, and beverage) complete with each meal's own time chart so you can prepare for your next grill party or intimate dinner for two with the least amount of anxiety.

Grill, Utensils, and Accessories

Let's start with the grill. Quite frankly, there is only one grill worth purchasing—the charcoal kettle grill—the round, fat, egg-shaped grill with a removable lid. This grill is relatively inexpensive, simple to use, accommodates recipes requiring wood smoking, and is easy to clean. What more can you ask for in a grill?

Think twice before purchasing a propane grill. Sure, it's easy to light—just a flick of a switch and it's ready to use in ten minutes rather than the twenty-five minutes that is required for charcoal—but the gas grill is more expensive, requires refilling of the propane tank, cannot match the heat intensity of a charcoal grill, doesn't

lend itself to wood smoking, and, most importantly, doesn't produce a grill taste nearly as savory as that of a charcoal grill. If you are going to go through the effort of using a grill, most likely because you are having family or friends over to your home, then give them a real treat. Remember, your guests may not eat grilled food very often, so when they are invited to a backyard barbecue they are expecting the sights, sounds, and tastes of a *real* backyard barbecue!

There are different sizes of the charcoal kettle grill If you don't already own one then look for the twenty-two inch size (I will explain why shortly), and one with the lever attached to the bottom of the grill so that you can sweep the ashes directly into a collecting pan. The lever is on the outside of the grill so clean-up is not only fast but accomplished without having to touch the ashes.

The next item to purchase is a cast iron grill-top upon which the food is placed for grilling. It is made exclusively for the 22-inch kettle grill. This separate grill-top has a large middle section made of cast-iron and smaller outside sections made of aluminum.

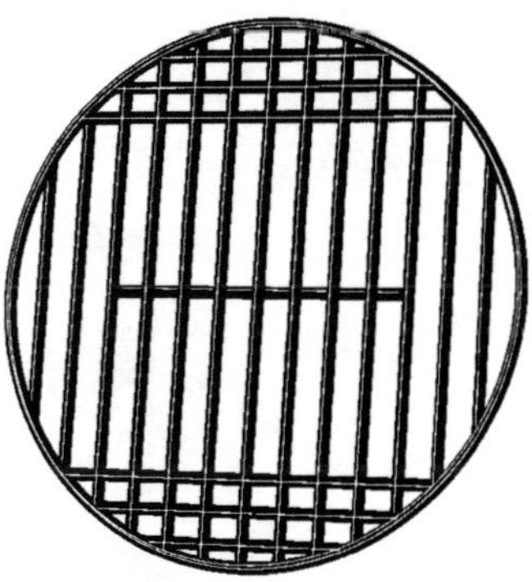

Opposite sides of the outside aluminum sections are hinged to allow additional charcoal, or wood chips for smoking, to be added without having to pick up the entire grill-top and everything on it. These hinges come in very handy when grilling your Thanksgiving turkey (see page 91).

A third essential purchase is a "chimney" to start the fire. The chimney is one of the greatest inventions in grilling history. All you need do to is crumple two full sheets of newspaper and add them to the bottom of the chimney. Then, you turn the chimney right-side up and add your charcoal. A perforated metal plate separates the charcoal from the newspaper yet allows the fire from the ignited newspaper to reach the charcoal. Once a flame is visible above the pile of charcoal sitting in the chimney (usually twenty-five minutes after lighting the newspaper) the charcoal is ready. You then pick up the chimney (of course, it has a nice wooden handle) and empty the charcoal onto the lower grate of the grill. *Voila!* You're ready for grilling. By the way, don't hold me to the twenty-five minutes with the chimney—in January it may take more than twenty-five minutes, a chimney crammed full of charcoal also

may take more than twenty-five minutes, and if it is raining it may take twenty-five hours!

With respect to rain and backyard grilling parties—they obviously do not go together; however, from time-to-time having the two occur simultaneously is unavoidable. Either you have planned a special celebration that must go on rain or shine, or the rain develops late in the day after all of your guests have arrived. While I can't offer any solace with respect to dampened spirits (as well as dampened clothes) I can offer some encouragement that the food you bought will not go to waste, can still be grilled, and with a taste just as great as expected. Recently, I had the misfortune of planning a grilling party only to have a hard-driving rain arrive just as I was lighting the chimney. I was determined to serve grilled food, even if it meant my getting wet (my guests were dry and just as comfortable inside my house as they were outside before the rain started). To get the chimney lit, I held the lid of the grill about one foot above the chimney as I was lighting the newspaper. When the newspaper was lit, I placed the chimney on the lower grate and covered the grill with the lid making sure that the bottom and top vents were open and that the top vent was not directly above the chimney, thus preventing the rain from falling on and dampening the charcoal. It worked! Thirty-five minutes later the coals were hot and ready for grilling. While the chimney took ten minutes longer than normal and the lid had to be used during grilling to keep the rain from snuffing out the fire, both were a small price to pay for a hot fire on a rainy day!

The chimney also solves the problem of how much charcoal to use for a standard grilled meal. My rule of thumb is that if the total grill time is short, say fifteen minutes for the appetizer and fifteen to thirty minutes for the entree and vegetables (total of thirty to forty-five minutes), then I would fill it three-quarters full. Any longer grill time and you should fill it completely, keeping in mind that after forty-five minutes you will need to add more charcoal to keep the temperature of the fire at the ideal heat intensity.

With respect to charcoal, just purchase the standard charcoal briquettes. A twenty pound bag is economical and lasts a long time. I really don't think you get much better taste with the more expensive hardwoods.

Finally, purchase a good spatula with a long handle, a pair of tongs, meat thermometers (standard and instant read), metal or bamboo skewers, and oven mitts. Also, a stiff wire brush is a necessity for keeping the grill-top clean.

In summary, here is a list of everything that you will need for your minimalist journey to simple but elegant backyard grilling:

- kettle grill (twenty-two inch diameter)
- cast iron grill-top (twenty-two inch diameter)
- chimney
- charcoal briquettes (twenty pound bag)
- spatula
- tongs
- meat thermometers (standard and instant read)
- pair of oven mitts
- skewers
- stiff wire brush

Let the fun begin!!

The Fire

Once you have the charcoal briquettes in the chimney glowing hot, then you need to determine which of the two types of fires to build: **direct** (charcoal in the middle of the grill) or **indirect** (charcoal on two sides of the grill and opposite one another).

If you are going to cook something for more than one-half hour (for example, turkey, pork roast, or smoked fish), use the indirect method. As a rule of thumb, the indirect method goes hand-in-hand with using the grill cover or the lid. The reason for the indirect method and the lid is that you are cooking a thick piece of meat and you need to make sure that the inside gets cooked as well as the outside; or, you are smoking meat or fish and you need to be assured that the smoky flavor is working its way around and into what you are grilling.

For all other types of food, use the direct method. As you may suspect, the direct method goes hand-in-hand with not using the lid. With the direct method, you are cooking a thin piece of meat or you have decided not to smoke the meat or fish but to simply impart a "charred" taste to the food. It is this charred taste that is distinctive to direct method grilling. You may want to use the lid with a direct fire to prevent a flare-up when the meat being grilled contains enough fat that a grease fire may develop.

One other benefit of a direct fire is the impact it has on the presentation of the food. Have you ever dined at a really nice restaurant and ordered a thick, juicy steak? When it is brought out it looks too good to eat: the grill marks have the distinctive cross-hatching, and the meat or fish is charred on the outside but the inside is juicy and tender. A direct fire with a cast iron grill-top will achieve the same results—the searing process will lock in the juices while adding a crispy outside. And, I will let you in on a little secret—the cross-hatched grill marks are created by lifting and rotating the food *before* turning it. Trust me! It works! When the food has been removed from the grill, serve it right-side up and you will have a perfectly prepared and beautifully presented dish.

Direct Versus Indirect Fires

A direct fire has charcoal spread evenly under the grilled food and heats the food "directly" from below. An indirect fire has charcoal lumped evenly into two sections on opposite sides of the grill with no charcoal in the center of the grill. In this method, the heat

Direct Fire

Indirect Fire

comes to the food "indirectly" from the sides and from the lid. A direct fire delivers high temperatures to the food: the heat source is near the food and the absence of the lid provides the fire with the greatest amount of oxygen. A direct fire will cook the outside of the food more than the inside—ideal with steaks, hamburgers, chops, and most fish, vegetables, and appetizers—and will cook the food quickly. The indirect method creates a cooler fire and fairly evenly cooks the inside as well as the outside of the food. With the lid on, you can more easily control cooking temperatures, which is very important if you are grilling for a few hours—such as when you grill your turkey on Thanksgiving Day (see page 91)!

Impact of Vents

One final point about the fire. There are two sets of vents for air to enter or escape—one set at the bottom of the grill and one set on the lid. The set at the bottom is easy to use—always leave it fully-open until you are finished grilling. Once finished, then close both sets of vents. With the lid replaced the fire will become extinguished very quickly due to the lack of oxygen. You don't need to douse the fire with water and you can reuse the charcoal the next time you grill.

The trickier vent is the one on the lid. With the lower vent always open when grilling, the upper vent will control the temperature of the fire. You will be amazed at how quickly the fire will die down when you close the upper vent. For example, if you are grilling hamburgers using a direct fire and experience flare-ups from fat dripping onto the hot coals, you can use the lid with a closed vent to quickly reduce the temperature of the fire.

Unless you are trying to extinguish or tame a fire that is out of control, I would leave the top vent fully open to half-open. A fully closed top vent will not put out the fire if the bottom vent is open, but it will reduce the heat to a level so low that the food may cook too slowly.

Always use fresh charcoal in the chimney. Before starting the chimney, simply knock the gray ash off the used charcoal and leave it on the lower grate. When the fresh charcoal comes in contact with the used charcoal, the used charcoal will automatically light.

I hope that you appreciate the benefits of both the direct and indirect cooking methods. To help you perfect your grilled meal, each recipe will highlight the following: type of fire (direct or indirect) whether or not to use the lid, and the total grill time.

Now you know your fire!

The Smoke

If you are new to grilling or have never used wood chips you may feel tempted to skip this section. Don't! It is not as mysterious as you may think. While wood smoking is not a science but an art, it will take very little practice before you are creating elegant wood smoked meals.

The smoking of certain foods—and I emphasize certain foods—imparts a subtlety that can turn a simple meal into a very memorable occasion for both you and your guests. Not only is the taste unusual and seldom encountered, but the smoke emanating from the grill will add that extra touch of magic that will captivate your guests.

Not every edible plant, animal, or fish should be smoked. For example, I think that smoking a good steak or pork tenderloin is a mistake: It is a waste of time to smoke anything that has a wonderful flavor all its own, has been marinated, or is to be covered with a heavy sauce. The subtlety of the smoke flavor is either not needed, detracts from the natural grilled flavor, or will be hidden by other much stronger flavors. Only a small number of the recipes in this handbook call for wood smoking. In all cases, the lid is used and an indirect fire is required. Each recipe in this handbook states whether smoking is recommended and what type of wood to use.

I suggest that you buy three types of wood chips: **hickory, mesquite, and apple.** Hickory is the most universal wood for smoking; mesquite the most pungent;

and apple imparts a sweet taste. These woods come in small bags either as chips or large chunks. The chips are easier to use but the chunks last longer.

No matter which wood you select or whether you select chips or chunks, you must soak them in water for at least thirty minutes before you drain them and add them to the fire. If you don't soak them properly they will not smoke but simply catch fire and quickly burn out. By the way, you can't over soak the chip; they can retain only so much water. To add the chips to the fire, simply lift up the grates on the sides of the grill-top, drain the chips, and sprinkle them on top of the charcoal. Cover with the lid and you are ready to smoke.

I would recommend that you sprinkle one handful over each of the two mounds of charcoal arranged for the indirect fire. Add extra chips whenever the smoke has stopped and the food still needs additional smoking time—about every thirty minutes.

Grilling with wood chips takes longer than if no wood chips are used: it takes time for the smoke flavor to permeate the meat or fish. And, in keeping with the minimalist theme, I would not recommend wood smoking if I did not think that it is relatively simple, significantly enhances the taste of the food, and further complements your backyard grilling festivities.

Now you know the smoking techniques—use them!

Recipes

The following sections contain my favorite minimalist recipes. Most of these seventy-five plus recipes have a very short, if any, grill time—with the exception of six which take more than one hour—and most need little preparation time and few ingredients (the ingredients are bolded in each recipe). While some of the recipes contain more fat and calories than others, all of the recipes are healthful. All of the cuts of beef, pork, lamb, and chicken should be purchased lean with much of any remaining fat expected to be rendered during grilling. Additional ingredients are recommended only when necessary to tenderize or add flavor. Occasionally, a recipe will call for a favorite marinara sauce or cocktail sauce only because to attempt to duplicate their great tastes with homemade versions that take days of preparation would violate the minimalist goal of this handbook—elegance in simplicity.

The recipes selected for each section are intentionally broad to accommodate a variety of tastes. The Appetizer Section has recipes including fish, breads, soups, and salsa to accompany chips. The Vegetables Section contains recipes for just about every vegetable that can be grilled. Each Entree Section contains at least one wood smoked recipe, a barbecue-sauced entree (excluding fish), a marinated entree, and a sandwich recipe (excluding fish).

Special occasions are the best times to treat your family and guests to a grilled meal which, because of its unique taste and presentation, should be memorable for all. Once you grill your first Thanksgiving Day turkey, your family will never let another Thanksgiving Day pass without a turkey grilling in the backyard, with its wonderful wood smoke scent penetrating the house and neighborhood. For festive summer occasions like Independence Day, beautifully prepared pulled beef sandwiches served with a hint of barbecue sauce and side dishes of cole slaw and baked beans cannot be matched.

I hope that your grilling experiences will be as rewarding as mine have been, and I hope that your family and guests enjoy your minimalist meals.

Appetizers

Appetizers

Appetizers are perhaps the most important course served during a grilling party. They set the mood and the expectations of your guests. Appetizers begin the grilling process with all the fire, smoke, and aromas one expects to experience during a grilling get-together. Appetizers beckon your guests to the grill to watch for themselves your grilling expertise in action. As you know, it is nearly impossible to attend a cookout and not be lured by the sights, sounds, and smells of a hot grill.

Since it is the appetizer that sets the mood, care should be taken in pairing the right appetizer with the entree. While an inappropriate appetizer selection for a given entree is not disastrous, a carefully planned meal can maximize the enjoyment of the food. You should have little difficulty selecting the appropriate appetizers given the number and variety included in this handbook.

All of the appetizers are simple to prepare, most involve few ingredients, and all require little grilling effort and attention. With but one exception, very little grill time is required, so the coals should remain sufficiently hot for the grilling of most entrees without the addition of extra charcoal. Of course, the entree should be grilling only while you and your guests are enjoying the beautifully cooked appetizers.

Appetizer Recipes

Recipe	Preparation + Grill Time under 30 min.	Grill Time Under 20 min.	Loved by Children	Best with Wood Smoke
Smoked Trout			?	X
Grilled Portobello Mushrooms	X	X		
Grilled Bruschetta		X	?	
Grilled Quesadilla	X	X	X	?
Wood-Smoked Pizza	X	X	X	X
Grilled Nachos	X	X	X	
Grilled Clams	X	X		
Grilled Shrimp Cocktail		X	?	
Grilled Crab Cakes	X	X	?	
Grilled Polenta		X	X	
Gazpacho Soup	NA	NA	?	
Summer Salsa	NA	NA	?	

Smoked Trout

My favorite of all appetizers! Simply the most elegant and unusual to serve despite the grilling time required to infuse a thin fish with wood smoke. I hope that you will find this the most gracious of all appetizers and one that your family and guests will remember for a long time.

Purchase as many **whole fresh trout** as you would like to serve, keeping in mind that one trout will serve 2 to 3 people. Have the head and scales removed and the fish deboned and sliced open.

Add the fish to a shallow pan with **2 quarts of cold water** and **1/4 cup of coarse salt.** Cover and place in the refrigerator for 2 to 4 hours. This will firm up the flesh of the fish.

When you are ready for grilling, remove the fish from the salt water, rinse under cold water, and pat dry. Apply a **light coat of olive oil** to the skin side of the trout so that it will not stick to the grill during cooking. **Add pepper to taste** to the nonskin side of the fish.

Add the trout, skin side down, to the middle of an indirect fire. Add hickory wood chips to the coals and cover with the lid. Let it cook for 30 to 40 minutes, or until the flesh of the fish begins to pull away from the skin.

Remove from the grill and, with a sharp knife, cut the meat away from the skin. Slice into small bite-sized pieces and serve immediately with crackers.

Fire: indirect
Lid: covered
Wood Smoke: hickory
Total Grill Time: 30 to 40 minutes
Servings: 1 trout for 2 to 3 people

Grilled Portobello Mushrooms

The wonderful earthy flavor of these mushrooms is enhanced by the aroma of the charcoal grill. In addition, the short preparation and grilling times and the ease of serving make this a true minimalist recipe.

Remove the stems from as many **portobello mushrooms** as you would like to serve, keeping in mind that 1 medium-size mushroom will serve 1 person. Rinse under cold water and pat dry. Brush both sides with **olive oil** and add **salt and pepper to taste.**

Place on the grill directly over the coals of a direct or indirect fire for 5 minutes. Turn over and grill for another 5 minutes. Remove from the grill and serve immediately.

It couldn't be any easier or lower in fat.

Fire: direct or indirect, whichever is used for the entree

Lid: uncovered

Wood Smoke: none

Total Grill Time: 10 minutes

Servings: 1 medium size mushroom per person

Grilled Bruschetta

This is an elegant and very light appetizer. Most of the effort for this dish is in its preparation which can be accomplished hours before your guests arrive. Also, it requires only 3 to 4 minutes of grill time allowing you to spend more time with your family and guests enjoying the backyard festivities.

This recipe comes in two parts: the topping for the garlic bread, and the garlic bread itself. Make the topping and the garlic oil, which will be added to the bread, at least 1 hour before the meal (and even 1 day ahead) to allow the ingredients to blend with each another. While any kind of **French or Italian loaves** will work well, the **small sourdough baguettes** are great tasting when grilled. Slice **one loaf of the bread** into 1/2 inch thick pieces just before grilling.

Grilled Garlic Bread: In a cup, combine **1/3 cup extra-virgin olive oil** and **2 teaspoons of minced garlic** (about 3 large garlic cloves). Let this oil mixture stand for at least 60 minutes before using. When ready to grill, paint each side of the bread slices with the garlic oil (reserving 3 tablespoons for the topping) and place on the grill directly over the coals of a direct or indirect fire. Grill for 1 to 2 minutes until slightly toasted. Turn over and grill for another 1 to 2 minutes. Remove the bread from the grill and transfer to a serving tray placed next to a bowl containing the topping (see below).

Topping: In a bowl, combine the following: **2 large fresh tomatoes (which have been peeled, seeded, and chopped), 1/3 cup of chopped white onion** (about 1/2 of 1 large onion), **1/2 cup of chopped fresh basil, 3 tablespoons of balsamic vinegar, 1/2 teaspoon of salt, 1/2 teaspoon of ground pepper,**

and 3 tablespoons of the garlic oil (see above). Let stand at least 60 minutes and then transfer to a serving bowl. Let your guests help themselves to spooning the topping onto the grilled bread.

Fire: direct or indirect, whichever is used for the entree
Lid: uncovered
Wood Smoke: none
Total Grill Time: 3 to 4 minutes
Servings: 1 small loaf for 6 to 8 people

Grilled Quesadilla

An appetizer that is very simple to prepare and can accommodate large parties with ease. The grill time is very short and several quesadillas can be grilled at one time. This appetizer tastes great with or without wood smoking, so follow the lead of your entree when preparing the fire and using wood chips.

Purchase **1 package of flour tortillas** (about 10 per package) and **2 packages of diced Monterey Jack cheese** (8 ounces per package). While optional, I would recommend that you purchase **1 bunch of scallions** and **3 jalapeño peppers** to add some spiciness.

Between 2 tortillas, add a handful of cheese, a few diced scallions, and a few thin slices of jalapeño peppers, with the seeds removed (the peppers should be sliced crosswise). Repeat the above steps until all the tortillas, cheese, and peppers have been used.

Place the quesadillas, 3 at a time, onto the grill directly over the coals of a direct or indirect fire. After they have become slightly toasted, about 3 to 4 minutes, turn and grill for another 3 to 4 minutes, making sure that the cheese has melted. Remove from the grill and slice into 6 or 8 pieces per quesadilla. Remove and serve immediately. As an option, serve your **favorite salsa** (bottled or freshly prepared Summer Salsa, see page 40) on the side for dipping.

Fire: direct or indirect, whichever is used for the entree
Lid: uncovered
Wood Smoke: Not necessary but can use hickory or mesquite wood
Total Grill Time: 6 to 8 minutes
Servings: 10 to 12 (3 slices per serving)

Wood-Smoked Pizza

A favorite of children (as well as adults) for a variety of reasons: first, you can give into the children's wishes and let them make their own pizza; second, they can add whatever toppings they like; third, with the addition of the wood chips, the flavor is genuine wood smoke and rarely encountered at your local pizzeria; finally, because it is done in your backyard the clean-up is easy.

While this recipe is under the Appetizer Section, it can also be served as an entree.

For the crust, I would recommend either **frozen pizza dough or fresh dough** (see below), whichever you prefer. Also, the sauce can be any kind of **pizza sauce** you prefer. As for the cheese, I would suggest slices of **provolone cheese** (however, you may also use **shredded mozzarella cheese, shredded Monterey Jack cheese,** or slices of **goat cheese).**

There are two secrets to grilling the pizza—a smoky flavor and a crispy crust. A commercially baked brick-oven pizza is nothing compared with the pizza created from a wood smoking grill. To create the smoke, I recommend hickory or mesquite chips.

The secret to creating a crispy crust is how you cook the dough. Begin by spreading the dough to the size of your pie pan. Without any sauce or cheese added, place the dough directly on the grill, over the coals of a direct or indirect fire, for 4 to 5 minutes, just to get one side slightly grilled. Remove the crust from the grill and turn it over such that the grilled side is facing up. For each 10 to 12 inch round pizza, **add 1/3 can of 12-ounce pizza sauce** and **4 to 6 ounces of cheese.** Add **your favorite toppings in any amount.**

Put the pizza back on the grill, cover with the lid, and cook for 7 to 8 minutes.

Remove from the grill and let stand 2 to 3 minutes until the cheese is firm. Slice and serve.

Fresh Pizza Dough

Add **1 package of active dry yeast** to **1 cup of warm water**. To a food processor add **2 1/2 cups of unbleached all-purpose flour** and **1 teaspoon of salt.** With the motor running slowly add the warm water and **1 tablespoon of olive oil**. Process the mixture until 1 or 2 balls of dough are formed. Remove the dough from the processor, place on a lightly-floured surface, and knead for 5 minutes. Transfer to a bowl that has been lightly coated with olive oil. Cover the bowl with a damp kitchen towel and let rest at room temperature. After 1 hour the dough should be double in size; knead the dough again for 5 minutes and separate into 2 balls. Again cover the balls with a damp kitchen towel for at least 20 minutes. Keep the balls covered for up to 2 hours, until ready to grill. Each ball of dough can be spread to fit the size of a 12-inch pie pan.

Fire: direct or indirect, whichever is used for the entree
Lid: covered
Wood Smoke: hickory or mesquite wood
Total Grill Time: 11 to 13 minutes
Servings: 1 pizza for 4 to 6 people served as an appetizer

Grilled Nachos

This version is even better tasting than its cousins served in Mexican restaurants due to the charcoal grilling. The melted cheese and tortilla chips are infused with the charcoal fire aroma which makes this an especially appealing appetizer, not to mention the very easy preparation and short grilling time.

Purchase one bag of **unseasoned tortilla chips** and spread the chips onto a sheet of aluminum foil about the size of a cookie sheet. Add enough chips so that no foil is showing from underneath the layer of chips. Sprinkle **1 package (8 ounces) of shredded Monterey Jack cheese** evenly over the chips. Add thin slices of **scallions (1 bunch)** to the chips. As an option, add thin slices of **jalapeno peppers (up to 3 peppers)** to the chips along with the scallions.

Place the sheet of foil containing the chips and cheese on the grill of a direct or indirect fire (it need not be placed directly over the coals) and cover with the lid. Grill for 10 minutes or until the cheese has melted. Make sure to watch the nachos closely as the cheese will burn if left on the grill too long. Remove and serve immediately. As an option, serve your **favorite bottled salsa** (or freshly prepared Summer Salsa, see page 40) on the side for dipping.

Fire: direct or indirect, whichever is used for the entree
Lid: covered
Wood Smoke: none needed
Total Grill Time: 10 minutes
Servings: 4 to 6

Grilled Clams

A very simple appetizer to prepare, and one with a wonderful taste and an equally enchanting presentation. Your guests will love the opened shells with their grill-smoke infused meat.

Purchase **enough fresh hard-shell clams** such that each person will be served 3 to 4 clams. Rinse the clams under cold water to remove any sand and debris. Place the clams in a container and cover with cold water. For every **2 quarts of cold water** used to soak the clams add **1/4 cup of coarse salt** and **1/4 cup of cornmeal** (optional). The salt and cornmeal will aid in further removing any sand and debris that may be in the clams. Cover and place in the refrigerator (or store in a cool place) for 3 to 4 hours.

Before grilling, remove the clams from the water bath and rinse under cold water. Discard any clams with shells that are open. Place the unopened clams on the grill, directly over the coals of a direct or indirect fire, and cook for 5 minutes. Turn over and grill for another 5 minutes. Remove the clams from the grill, discard any clams with shells still unopened, and serve immediately with **melted butter** (optional).

Fire: direct or indirect, whichever is used for the entree
Lid: uncovered or covered
Wood Smoke: none
Total Grill Time: 10 minutes
Servings: 3 to 4 clams per person

Grilled Shrimp Cocktail

A simple variation on the traditional shrimp cocktail. One of the easiest appetizers to prepare and one of the most desired by guests.

Prepare and grill **1-1/2 pounds of large shrimp** following the recipe for Grilled Shrimp in the Entree Section (see page 107). When cooked, remove immediately from the grill and place the shrimp on a serving plate next to a bowl containing **lemon wedges** and your **favorite bottled cocktail sauce.** With toothpicks, simply have your guests dip the shrimp into the cocktail sauce—it's that easy.

Fire: direct or indirect, whichever is used for the entree
Lid: uncovered
Wood Smoke: none
Total Grill Time: 8 to 10 minutes
Servings: 8 to 10

Grilled Crab Cakes

This is one of the easiest of the appetizers to prepare and one of the fastest to grill. There is no preparation time involved and the grilling can't be any more straightforward. And, of course, the taste is wonderful.

While the recipe is under the Appetizer Section, it can also be served as an entree.

Purchase already prepared but **fresh crab cakes** (allowing one per person) from your local fish market.

Place the crab cakes on the grill directly over the coals of a direct or indirect fire for 8 to 10 minutes. Turn and grill for an additional 5 minutes. Remove and serve immediately with your favorite **store-bought cocktail sauce** (optional).

Fire: direct or indirect, whichever is used for the entree
Lid: uncovered
Wood Smoke: none
Total Grill Time: 13 to 15 minutes
Servings: 1 crab cake per person served as an appetizer

Grilled Polenta

This is a great tasting appetizer your guests most likely have never been served. Not only is it a rare taste treat, the preparation is easy, and the grill time is short.

In a saucepan bring to a boil **2 cups** (or one 14 ounce can) **of chicken broth.** While the chicken broth is being heated, whisk **1 cup of cornmeal** into 1 cup of cold water. Once the chicken broth has reached boiling, add the cornmeal mixture. Reduce the heat to low and cook, stirring continuously until the mixture pulls away from the sides of the saucepan—about 15 minutes. Stir in **3 tablespoons of butter** and **1 teaspoon of ground pepper. Season to taste with salt.**

Pour the mixture into a buttered 10 to 12 inch pie pan (a smaller pie pan will create a thicker polenta). Let cool for thirty minutes and then cover and refrigerate for 3 to 4 hours.

When ready to grill, cut the polenta into 8 to 12 slices and brush both the top and the bottom of each slice with **olive oil** (optional). Place the sliced polenta on the grill, directly over the coals of a direct or indirect fire, for 6 to 7 minutes, until slightly browned. Turn over and grill for another 6 to 7 minutes. Serve immediately. Include a side dish of warm **marinara sauce** for dipping (optional).

Fire: direct or indirect, whichever is used for the entree
Lid: uncovered
Wood Smoke: none necessary, but can use hickory or mesquite wood
Total Grill Time: 12 to 14 minutes
Servings: 8 to 12

Gazpacho Soup

This is the classic soup for a summer grilling party. It is refreshing, requires no grilling, and is offered during the hot summer months. It can be served instead of, or along with, an appetizer. Since it is a summer soup, take the additional time to use the fresh vegetables of the summer rather than their canned cousins.

Plan to make this soup several hours before your guests arrive so that the flavors have time to combine with one another and the soup has time to chill.

Using a food processor, chop **1/2 of a medium-size white onion, 1 medium-size cucumber,** and **3 large red tomatoes** (which have been peeled). Then mix in: **1 teaspoon of minced garlic** (2 garlic cloves), **1/3 cup of tomato juice, 1/4 cup of olive oil,** and **1-1/2 teaspoons of liquid hot pepper sauce.** Add **salt to taste** and **additional tomato juice** if soup is too thick. Refrigerate for 3 to 4 hours before serving.

(The easiest way to peel the tomatoes is to place them in boiling water for 30 to 60 seconds, remove, and immediately immerse them in an ice water bath to stop the cooking process. The skins can then be removed with little effort.)

Fire: na
Lid: na
Wood Smoke: na
Total Grill Time: na
Servings: 6

Summer Salsa
(to accompany tortilla chips)

I first tasted homemade salsa when my friend Patti brought it to one of my backyard parties. It had a very pleasant consistency, contained the freshest of vegetables, and had just enough spiciness that the children enjoyed it as much as the adults. While the number of ingredients is slightly larger than usual for this minimalist handbook, the fresh ingredients (at their peak during the summer months) create a taste far superior to the store-bought salsa versions. When paired with the tortillas chips, the combination creates a very successful beginning to any backyard get-together.

Using a food processor, chop **2 cups of fresh plum tomatoes** (which have been peeled) and **1/3 cup of sliced scallions** (about one bunch). Then mix in: **1 teaspoon of minced garlic** (2 garlic cloves), **2 tablespoons of chopped jalapeño peppers** (or more for added spiciness), **1 tablespoon of olive oil, 4 teaspoons of lime juice, 1/3 cup of fresh cilantro sprigs** (about 20 sprigs), and **salt to taste.** Refrigerate for 2 to 3 hours.

Serve with **unseasoned tortilla chips.** For a healthy alternative to the chips, place **corn tortillas** on the grill (purchase 1 package containing 10 tortillas) and warm each side for 2 to 3 minutes per side. Slice into wedge-shaped pieces and serve warm with the salsa.

Fire: na
Lid: na
Wood Smoke: na
Total Grill Time: na
Servings: 6 to 8

Vegetables

Vegetables

Certain vegetables are particularly well suited for grilling because their taste when slightly altered by the heat of the fire, is unusually sweet. For every one of the vegetable recipes in this handbook I recommend that you *not* use wood chips. The additional smoke will just detract from the wonderful taste of the vegetables. Also, I recommend that you keep the grill uncovered. A hot fire will bring out the best in the vegetables. Finally, depending on the type of fire needed for the entree, you can use either the direct or indirect method; however, grill the vegetables directly over the coals.

The vegetables should be served hot, so try to time the grilling with that of your entree. This means that you will need either to grill the vegetables simultaneously with the entree or grill them ahead of the entree and keep them warm either on a cool section of the grill-top or wrapped in aluminum foil.

Do not underestimate the appeal of grilled vegetables. Often I have had guests rave more about the taste of the grilled vegetables than the grilled entree, which took much longer to prepare and greater artistry to grill. On one particular occasion I served grilled bruschetta, grilled swordfish, and grilled corn to four couples. When dinner was over what do you think my guests raved about—the great taste of the grilled corn! Of course, that was the part of the meal that took no preparation time and little grilling acumen—requiring only the turning of the corn every few minutes to keep it from burning.

Vegetable Recipes

Recipe	Preparation + Grill Time under 30 min.	Grill Time Under 20 min.	Loved by Children	Best with Wood Smoke
Grilled Corn	X	X	X	
Grilled Potatoes		X	X	
Grilled Potato Chips	X	X	X	
Grilled Asparagus	X	X		
Grilled Broccoli	X	X	?	
Grilled String Beans	X	X	?	
Grilled Belgian Endive	X	X		
Grilled Scallions	X	X		
Grilled Onion	X	X		
Grilled Eggplant	X	X		

Grilled Corn

My favorite grilled vegetable. This could be the best part of an entire meal. In addition, it goes well with almost every entree, and, if prepared my way, is next to impossible to incorrectly grill.

Remove the husks and silk from **the corn,** rinse under cold water and pat dry. Add a small **amount of butter** to the corn lengthwise and then wrap each ear of corn in aluminum foil.

Place the foil-wrapped corn directly over the coals of a direct or indirect fire and make a 1/4 turn every 5 minutes. After about twenty minutes you should hear popping and hissing sounds. Remove 1 ear, open up the foil, and check to see that the corn has been slightly browned. If so, then it is ready.

If the entree is not yet ready, simply remove the ears of corn from the grill and keep them wrapped in foil. The foil will keep the corn hot for about fifteen minutes.

One nice thing about this recipe is that if you have a large party you can grill as many as twelve to fifteen ears of corn at once, covering the entire grill area. Once cooked, you can move them to the outside perimeter of the grill-top or even remove the ears completely and begin grilling the entree.

Fire: direct or indirect, whichever is used for the entree
Lid: uncovered
Wood Smoke: none
Total Grill Time: 20 minutes
Servings: 1 to 2 ears of corn per person

Grilled Potatoes

While the traditional baked potato is very popular to grill, I have a variation that is similar in taste, but has a crunchier exterior and takes less time to grill.

Slice large **Russet or Idaho potatoes** (one potato will serve 2 people) in half lengthwise and add to salted boiling water. Boil for 25 minutes. Remove from the water and pat dry.

Place on the grill directly over the coals of a direct or indirect fire. After 10 minutes turn over and grill for another 10 minutes until golden brown and crunchy. Remove from the grill and serve immediately. If the entree is not ready, then move the potatoes to a cool section of the grill or wrap in aluminum foil until ready. **Add salt to taste.** Serve with **butter or sour cream.**

Fire: direct or indirect, whichever is used for the entree
Lid: uncovered
Wood Smoke: none
Total Grill Time: 20 minutes
Servings: 1 large potato will serve two 2 people

Grilled Potato Chips

I think that this recipe is the best way to serve the basic potato and it is a sure-fire treat for all your guests. The taste approaches that of potato chips but without all the fat and calories.

Wash and peel **3 large Russet or Idaho potatoes.** Cut each into 1/8 inch thick slices crosswise and lay the slices flat between 2 sheets of paper towel. Press to remove any excess liquid. Lightly brush both sides of each slice with **olive oil** and sprinkle both sides with **coarse salt.**

Place on grill, directly over coals of a direct or indirect fire, and grill for approximately 7 to 8 minutes until golden brown on the bottom. Turn and grill for another 6 to 7 minutes. When both sides have browned and are crispy, move to the side of the grill to keep warm until the entree is ready. Remove and serve with entree.

Fire: direct or indirect, whichever is used for the entree
Lid: uncovered
Wood Smoke: none
Total Grill Time: 13 to 15 minutes
Servings: 4

Grilled Asparagus

Raw asparagus becomes sweet when grilled and is an ideal green vegetable to serve with an entree. In fact, it is one of just a few green vegetables that I recommend for grilling. Like most of the vegetable recipes, it is very simple to prepare and quick to grill.

Wash **asparagus spears** (allowing 4 spears per person) under cold water and remove the bottom 1 to 2 inches of each stalk. Place asparagus spears on the grill directly over the coals of a direct or indirect fire. Rotate every 3 minutes until they turn a dark green color. Remove from the grill after 10 to 12 minutes. **Add salt to taste.** If the entree is not ready, move the spears to a cooler section of the grill to keep warm.

Fire: direct or indirect, whichever is used for the entree
Lid: uncovered or covered
Wood Smoke: none
Total Grill Time: 10 to 12 minutes
Servings: 4 spears per person

Grilled Broccoli

This is one vegetable that I have avoided grilling until very recently and I must say that I regret not grilling it more often in the past. It is simple to prepare and tastes very different from steamed broccoli. When grilled, the florets take on a wonderful woodsy and smoked flavor which nicely complements most grilled entrees.

Several hours before grilling, cut **1 large bunch of broccoli** (about 1-1/2 pounds) into spears with 1- to 2-inch stems attached to the florets. Cook the broccoli in boiling salted water for 3 minutes. Immediately rinse under cold water to stop the cooking process. Drain and set aside at room temperature.

In a cup, combine **1/3 cup of extra-virgin olive oil** and **2 teaspoons of minced garlic** (about 3 large garlic cloves). Let this mixture stand for at least thirty minutes. When ready for grilling, pour the mixture over the broccoli and brush if necessary to coat completely.

Place the broccoli on the grill but not directly over the coals of a direct or indirect fire. Grill for 12 to 15 minutes (with or without the lid) turning occasionally until the color has deepened and the tips of the florets have turned brown. Remove and serve immediately or wrap in aluminum foil to keep warm until the entree is ready.

Fire: direct or indirect, whichever is used for the entree
Lid: uncovered or covered
Wood Smoke: none
Total Grill Time: 12 to 15 minutes
Servings: 1 bunch for 4 to 6 people

Grilled String Beans

A very easy vegetable to prepare and one that is impossible to incorrectly grill. The string beans absorb the grill aromas and become soft but still retain a slight crunch.

Snap **1-1/2 pounds of string beans** and rinse under cold water. Cook the beans in boiling salted water for 3 minutes. Immediately rinse under cold water to stop the cooking process. Drain and set aside at room temperature until ready for grilling.

Place the string beans on aluminum foil and set on the grill either directly over the coals of a direct or indirect fire or on the side. Grill for 20 minutes turning occasionally. Remove and serve immediately or wrap in aluminum foil to keep warm until the entree is ready.

Fire: direct or indirect, whichever is used for the entree
Lid: uncovered or covered
Wood Smoke: none, but can be used if wood smoking the entree
Total Grill Time: 20 minutes
Servings: 6

Grilled Belgian Endive

A simple vegetable that once grilled becomes alive with a subtle woodsy flavor. The outside leaves become crispy with a brown hue while the inside leaves remain moist and tender.

Slice each **Belgian endive** in half lengthwise and lightly coat all sides with **olive oil.**

Place on the grill, directly over the coals of a direct or indirect fire, and grill for 5 minutes. Turn over and grill for another 5 minutes. Remove from the grill, **add salt and pepper to taste,** and serve immediately with the entree.

Fire: direct or indirect, whichever is used for the entree

Lid: uncovered or covered

Wood Smoke: none, but can be used if wood smoking the entree

Total Grill Time: 10 minutes

Servings: 2 per whole endive

Grilled Scallions

The taste of this grilled vegetable is similar to that of grilled onions but with more subtlety. As with grilled onions, these can be served as a side vegetable or placed on top of grilled meat or fish. The dark color created by the grilling process is an appealing complement to most entrees.

Rinse a **bunch of scallions** under cold water, trim the ends, and lightly coat the stalks with **olive oil.**

Place on the grill, directly over the coals of a direct or indirect fire, and grill for 10 minutes, turning occasionally. Remove from the grill, add **salt to taste,** and serve immediately with the entree.

Fire: direct or indirect, whichever is used for the entree
Lid: uncovered or covered
Wood Smoke: none, but can be used if wood smoking the entree
Total Grill Time: 10 minutes
Servings: 4 per bunch of scallions

Grilled Onion

This is always a popular vegetable. It is quick, easy to prepare, and may accompany many different entrees. You can place the onion on top of the entree or use it as an accompaniment.

Cut **raw yellow or Vidalia onions** (allowing 1 onion for 2 people) into 1/2 inch slices and brush with a **small amount of olive oil.**

Place the onion directly over the coals of a direct or indirect fire and grill for 5 to 7 minutes. If you like, separate the inner circles of each slice to further brown the onion. Turn and grill for another 5 to 7 minutes. Remove and serve immediately. If the entree is not ready, you may move the onion to a cooler section of the grill to keep warm.

Fire: direct or indirect, whichever is used for the entree
Lid: uncovered
Wood Smoke: none
Total Grill Time: 10 to 14 minutes
Servings: 1 onion for 2 people

Grilled Eggplant

This easy-to-grill vegetable may be served as a side dish with an entree or as part of a vegetable sandwich. My wife places it on a roll with cheese and tomato for a great meatless sandwich.

Rinse the **eggplant** under cold water and pat dry. Cut into 3/4-inch thick slices. Add **olive oil** to both sides, and **salt and pepper to taste.**

Place on the grill, directly over the coals of a direct or indirect fire, and grill for 5 minutes. Turn over and grill for another 5 minutes. Remove immediately if served with an entree or let cool to be used in a sandwich at a later date. It will keep in the refrigerator for several days.

Fire: direct or indirect, whichever is used for the entree
Lid: uncovered
Wood Smoke: none
Total Grill Time: 10 minutes
Servings: 1 eggplant will serve 4 to 6 people

Beef

Beef Entrees

Beef dishes are the most versatile of entrees to grill. On one end of the spectrum are hamburgers, either simply grilled with the addition of just salt and pepper, or slightly more complex versions with a few added ingredients requiring little guesswork, little preparation, and a few short minutes of grilling. (The small amount of preparation time as well as the short grilling time are two very desirable attributes that should not be overlooked when grilling for large parties.)

In the center of the spectrum are steaks which, if grilled properly, are about as close to heaven as any food can get. Also, like hamburgers, steaks require little preparation time and a relatively short amount of grilling time, although they do require greater grilling expertise.

At the other end of the spectrum is brisket with its subtle texture and flavor, ideal for pulled beef sandwiches. Of course, there is also the fun side of beef—steak fajitas are less serious food but no less enjoyable to eat.

Whatever the occasion, from an informal cookout for a crowd, to an intimate dinner for two, to a festive gala with all the fixings, the following beef recipes will be guaranteed winners.

Beef Recipes

Recipe	Preparation + Grill Time under 30 min.	Grill Time Under 20 min.	Loved by Children	Best with Wood Smoke
Grilled Basic Hamburger	X	X	X	
Grilled Haute Cuisine Hamburger	X	X	X	
Smoked Hamburger	X		X	X
Grilled Hot Dogs	X	X	X	
Grilled Pulled Beef			X	
Grilled Steak Fajitas		X	X	
Grilled Teriyaki Flank Steak		X	X	
Grilled Filet Mignon	X	X	X	
Grilled Sirloin Steak	X	X	X	

Grilled Basic Hamburger

A nicely grilled hamburger seasoned with just salt and pepper is about the easiest possible entree to prepare (with the exception of the hot dog). It is an ideal entree for large parties because you can grill many at once, each batch only takes about ten minutes to grill, and the preparation time is very short. If the meat is grilled properly, your guests will enjoy what they have come to your cookout expecting—a hamburger seared on the outside, moist on the inside, beckoning each guest to add his or her favorite condiments.

Shape **1-1/2 pounds of 80 or 85% lean ground beef** into 6 patties and **add salt and pepper to taste.** For a slightly different taste, you may want to consider adding **3 dashes of Worcestershire sauce** to each side of the patties (which have been pricked on both sides with a fork) before they are placed on the grill.

Place the beef patties on the grill over a direct fire for 5 to 6 minutes, until each side is slightly charred. Turn and cook for an additional 4 to 5 minutes, adding 1 or 2 slices of your **favorite cheese** (optional). Cover with the lid to help melt the cheese. Remove from the grill and place on a traditional **hamburger bun.** Serve with your **favorite condiments.**

Fire: direct
Lid: uncovered
Wood Smoke: none
Total Grill Time: 9 to 11 minutes
Servings: 6 hamburgers

Grilled Haute Cuisine Hamburger

A slightly more challenging hamburger dish than the previous recipe, but still very easy to prepare. The addition of shallots and tarragon elevates the basic hamburger to a new level of elegance without abandoning simplicity, thus preserving our minimalist goals.

I hope that you will agree that this is a true "haute cuisine" hamburger that can be created with few ingredients and little preparation and grilling.

To **1-1/2 pounds of 80 or 85% lean ground beef** add **3/4 cup of bread crumbs** (which can be toasted bread cut into small pieces), **1 diced shallot** (3 tablespoons), and **2 teaspoons of dried tarragon.** Mix well but don't overmix or the meat will become tough. Shape into 6 patties and season both sides of each patty with **salt and pepper to taste.**

Place the beef patties on the grill over a direct fire for 5 to 6 minutes, until each bottom is slightly charred. Turn and cook for an additional 4 to 5 minutes adding your **favorite cheese** (optional). Cover with the lid to help melt the cheese. Remove from the grill and place on either a traditional **hamburger bun** or a toasted **English muffin** for something different. Serve with your **favorite condiments.**

Fire: direct
Lid: uncovered
Wood Smoke: none
Total Grill Time: 9 to 11 minutes
Servings: 6 hamburgers

Smoked Hamburger

A nice variation on the basic hamburger that can still accommodate large parties. In fact, the smoke billowing from the grill adds an extra touch of mystery and anticipation to any backyard get-together.

The hickory or mesquite wood will infuse the ground beef with just the right amount of sweetness and subtlety.

Shape **1-1/2 pounds of 80 or 85% lean ground beef** into 6 patties and add **salt and pepper to taste.**

Place the beef patties in the middle of the grill over an indirect fire to which you've added hickory or mesquite wood chips. Replace the lid and grill for 10 minutes. Turn over and grill for an additional 10 minutes. Remove from the grill, place on a **hamburger bun,** and serve with your **favorite condiments.**

Fire: indirect
Lid: covered
Wood Smoke: hickory or mesquite
Total Grill Time: 20 minutes
Servings: 6 hamburgers

Grilled Hot Dogs

The most ubiquitous grilled dish. You can't have a grilling party, invite children, and not grill hot dogs. Even though hot dogs may not be inspiring, they are easy to cook and kids love them.

The two keys to great hot dogs are **fresh butcher-quality hot dogs** and a hot direct fire.

Place the hot dogs directly over the coals of a direct or indirect fire and quickly char the outside which, if done quickly, will leave the inside moist and juicy. Don't pierce them and don't slice them open before you grill them or they will dry out. After 5 to 7 minutes, with periodic turning, remove from the grill and place in your standard **hot dog bun.** Serve with your **favorite condiments.**

There is no better grilled hot dog than one slightly crunchy on the outside and tender and juicy on the inside.

By the way, don't use wood chips with hot dogs. The wood smoke will interfere with the spices in the hot dog and the hot dog will develop a funny taste.

Fire: direct or indirect fire
Lid: uncovered
Wood Smoke: none
Total Grill Time: 5 to 7 minutes
Servings: 1 per hot dog

Grilled Pulled Beef Sandwiches

This recipe is very similar to the Grilled Pulled Pork recipe in the Pork and Lamb Entree section (see page 79). The meal is very informal, since the beef is mixed with barbecue sauce and then served to each guest on hamburger buns. The taste is true barbecue.

This meal tastes just as good, if not better, the next day. If you think that you will be in a rush the day of your get-together, then grill the meat, pull it into shreds, and refrigerate the day before your party.

Purchase from your butcher **4 pounds of beef brisket (first cut).** Rinse the meat under cold water, pat dry, and rub all sides of the meat with **2 teaspoons of minced garlic (3 large garlic cloves)** and sprinkle with **coarse salt and ground pepper.**

Place the brisket in the middle of the grill over an indirect fire. Cover with the lid and turn the top vent to the 3/4 open position to lower the temperature of the fire and slow the cooking process. When the internal temperature of the meat equals 170 to 175 degrees (approximately 1-1/2 hours) remove from the grill, let it sit for 1 hour at room temperature, and then pull the meat into shreds making sure to discard any fat and charred, hard-to-chew pieces. (At this point, you may refrigerate the shredded meat and reheat the following day.)

Warm some **barbecue sauce** (see below) in a saucepan (make sure to reserve 1 cup of the sauce to be served on the side with the sandwiches). Place the shredded meat (either just pulled or pulled the previous day and refrigerated) in the barbecue sauce. Spoon the beef shreds onto **hamburger buns** and serve immediately.

Many of the barbecue sauces available at your local

grocery store are great tasting and, of course, require no preparation. In keeping with the minimalist theme of this handbook, I cannot recommend against using these sauces; however, I have found that these store-bought versions are not delicate enough for this recipe or any recipe in which the sauce is to be added only after the meat is removed from the grill. As such, I have included the following sauce recipe which is slightly spicy but still delicate enough to complement the beef without overwhelming it. In addition, this sauce recipe requires few ingredients and is easy to prepare.

Barbecue Sauce

In a medium-size saucepan combine the following: **1/2 cup of finely chopped white onion** (1 medium size chopped onion), **1-1/2 cups of ketchup**, **1/3 cup of red wine vinegar, 1/2 cup of beer** (you can substitute 1/2 cup of water for the beer), **1-1/2 tablespoons of Worcestershire sauce,** and **1-1/2 teaspoons of liquid hot pepper sauce.** Bring to a boil, reduce heat and simmer for approximately 15 minutes, allowing the sauce to slightly thicken. Reserve one cup of the sauce and combine the beef shreds with the remaining sauce. Serve immediately with the reserved sauce on the side.

Fire: indirect
Lid: covered
Wood Smoke: none
Total Grill Time: 1-1/2 hours
Servings: 14 to 16 sandwiches

Grilled Steak Fajitas

This is a very festive recipe that lets your imagination run wild in selecting side accompaniments, appetizers, and beverages. Although the meat does need to marinate for several hours, the preparation time for the marinade is short, as is the grill time. I am confident that you and your guests will enjoy the taste almost as much as creating an individualized meal with the various accompaniments.

Purchase from your butcher **2-1/2 to 3 pounds of skirt steak.** Rinse the meat under cold water and pat dry. Rub both sides with **ground black pepper.** Coat the meat with **1-1/2 cups of lime juice,** cover, and refrigerate for 2 to 3 hours.

One hour before grilling, remove the steak from the refrigerator and let stand at room temperature. Remove the meat from the lime juice and pat dry. Discard the lime juice. Season both sides of the meat with **coarse salt.** Before grilling the meat, place **flour tortillas** (purchase 2 packages, each package containing 10 tortillas) on the grill for 2 to 3 minutes (turning once) to warm, making sure that they do not overcook (or they will become crispy and difficult to fold once you add the meat). Remove the tortillas from the grill and wrap in aluminum foil to keep warm until you are ready to serve.

Place the meat on the grill over a direct fire for 9 to 10 minutes, turn and grill for another 9 to 10 minutes. Remove from the grill, let sit for 2 to 3 minutes to retain the juices, and cut against the grain into 1/4-inch thick slices.

Add a few slices of the meat to each of the tortillas and serve with shredded **Monterey Jack cheese** (purchase two 8-ounce packages), **finely chopped red or**

white onion (2 medium size chopped onions), and **diced tomatoes** (2 large diced tomatoes), or your **favorite bottled salsa** or make your own freshly prepared Summer Salsa (see page 40).

Fire: direct
Lid: uncovered
Wood Smoke: none
Total Grill Time: 18 to 20 minutes
Servings: 8

Grilled Teriyaki Flank Steak

This is a great tasting entree with a short grill time; however, the marinade time is long—overnight. This marinade allows an otherwise tough cut of meat to become tender and juicy.

Wash and pat dry **2-1/2 pounds of flank steak (or London broil)** and place it in a nonreactive dish large enough to hold the beef. In a bowl combine: **1/3 cup of soy sauce, 1/4 cup of cooking sherry, 3 tablespoons of olive oil, 1/3 cup of chopped scallions** (about 1 bunch of scallions) and **2 teaspoons of minced garlic** (3 large garlic cloves). Add the marinade to the meat, cover, and refrigerate at least 12 hours and preferably overnight.

One hour before grilling, remove from the refrigerator and let stand at room temperature. Remove the meat from the marinade and pat dry. Discard the marinade. Place the meat on the grill over a direct fire for 10 minutes. Turn and grill for another 10 minutes. Remove from the grill, let stand for 5 minutes, and serve by slicing against the grain.

Fire: direct
Lid: uncovered
Wood Smoke: none
Total Grill Time: 20 minutes
Servings: 6

Grilled Filet Mignon

A good cut of beef tenderloin needs no embellishment. Simply add salt and pepper and you are ready to grill. The meat is tender and flavorful—no need to hide it with marinades and seasonings.

Have your butcher slice each **beef filet** to be 1-1/4 inches thick and weigh about 8 ounces. **Salt and pepper to taste** both sides of the filets.

Place the filets on the grill over a direct fire, and after 3 minutes rotate the meat 90 degrees without turning and let cook another 2 minutes. Turn and grill for another 3 to 4 minutes. Remove from the grill and place on a **toasted slice of bread** which has been cut to the size of the filet. Make sure that the side with the cross-hatched grill marks is facing upward on the plate. The design will impress your guests almost as much as the taste.

If you would like to add a little pizazz to the meal, use a **dollop of my Maitre d' Butter** (see below) which nicely complements the beef flavor without overwhelming the taste.

Maitre d' Butter

To **1/2 stick of room-temperature butter** add **1/2 teaspoon of dried onion, 1/2 teaspoon of dried parsley,** and **1/4 teaspoon of Worcestershire sauce.** Mix well. (This will serve 6 to 8 people.)

Fire: direct
Lid: uncovered
Wood Smoke: none
Total Grill Time: 8 to 9 minutes
Servings: 1 filet mignon per person

Grilled Sirloin Steak

This cut of beef, also called shell steak is cooked the same way as filet mignon. All you need is salt and pepper. No need to hide the wonderful taste with marinades and seasonings. Make sure to trim off any excess fat to avoid flare-ups which will singe the meat and perhaps impart a bad taste.

Purchase from your butcher **sirloin steaks,** each weighing about 8 ounces. Add **salt and pepper to taste.**

Place on the grill over a direct fire, and after about 3 minutes turn the meat 90 degrees and grill for another 2 minutes. Turn over and cook for another 3 to 4 minutes. Remove from the grill, remembering to serve the side with the cross-hatched grill marks facing upward on the plate.

If you wish to add a little pizazz to the dish, add a **dollop of my Maitre d' Butter** (see Grilled Filet Mignon Recipe on page 68), which nicely compliments the beef flavor without overwhelming the taste.

Fire: direct
Lid: uncovered
Wood Smoke: none
Total Grill Time: 8 to 9 minutes
Servings: 1 steak per person

Pork and Lamb

Pork and Lamb Entrees

There is nothing more suitable to grilling and more easily transformed into a delectable entree than pork. Indeed, in my view, nothing tastes better than pork hot off the grill. A charcoal fire transforms pork from a rather mundane-looking piece of lean meat (and sometimes not so lean meat) into a beautifully colored and textured dish that has a glistening outer layer and a lean but still moist interior.

Unlike beef, pork is best prepared by bathing it in a marinade for several hours, coating the meat with sauce for spiciness, or smoking it for a few hours. No matter how it is prepared, the praise from your guests is universal and they won't be able to eat enough to satisfy their appetites.

Of all the meat entrees presented in this handbook, I have received the greatest compliments for my pork recipes. I think the reasons are that the preparation time is short, in most cases the grilling time is short, and what is brought to the table is so unlike what is normally eaten that the meal is truly a memorable treat for all involved.

The last entree that comes to mind when planning a grilling party is lamb. This is most likely due to a lack of familiarity with the different cuts of meat and the erroneous assumption that lamb has a gamy taste. I hope that these two recipes will convince you that neither is true and that lamb is a great tasting and rewarding treat that your guests rarely have the opportunity to enjoy.

Pork and Lamb Recipes

Recipe	Preparation + Grill Time under 30 min.	Grill Time Under 20 min.	Loved by Children	Best with Wood Smoke
Grilled Pork Tenderloin			X	
Grilled Pork Chops	X	X	X	
Herb-Smoked Pork Chops	X	X	X	X(herb)
Smoked Pork Roast			?	X
Grilled Pulled Pork Sandwiches			X	
Barbecue-Sauced Pork Ribs			X	
Grilled Leg of Lamb			?	
Grilled Lamb Chops	X	X	?	X(herb)

Grilled Pork Tenderloin

This is my favorite pork dish. It is also one of a handful of my recipes that uses a marinade that not only tenderizes but adds a taste that is unforgettable. In fact, this recipe has been passed around among my friends faster than any recipe in this book. I remember one meal in which I grilled this dish for four couples. Upon serving, all conversation came to a halt only to be continued once they'd eaten most of the meal. I considered their silence a great compliment and a good indication of a successful get-together.

Wash and pat dry **1-1/2 pounds of pork tenderloin** and place in a nonreactive dish. In a bowl whisk together: **1/4 cup of sugar, 2 tablespoons of ketchup, 2 tablespoons of soy sauce, 1 teaspoon of salt, 1/2 teaspoon of ground black pepper,** and **1/4 cup of canned chicken broth.** Coat the pork thoroughly with the marinade, cover, and let sit in the refrigerator for 6 to 8 hours, or overnight.

One hour before grilling, remove from the refrigerator and let stand at room temperature. Remove the meat from the marinade. Discard the marinade. Place the meat on the grill, over a direct fire, and cook for 15 minutes turning every 5 minutes. Transfer the meat so that it is not directly over the coals and cook for another 10 minutes. Slice into one of the tenderloins to check for doneness (it should be white or a very slight pink) and serve immediately.

Fire: direct
Lid: uncovered
Wood Smoke: none
Total Grill Time: 25 minutes
Servings: 4 to 6

Grilled Pork Chops

This is the easiest and fastest of the pork entrees to prepare and grill. Outside of the chops, no other ingredient is needed except salt and pepper. Once grilled, the outside of each chop becomes charred, but the inside meat remains moist—a recipe true to minimalist grilling.

Wash and pat dry **3 pounds of center-cut pork chops.** Add **salt and pepper to taste** to both sides.

Place the chops on the grill over a direct fire. Grill for 5 to 6 minutes, turn over, and grill the other side for 5 to 6 minutes longer. Remove from the grill and serve immediately.

Fire: direct
Lid: uncovered
Wood Smoke: none
Total Grill Time: 10 to 12 minutes
Servings: 4

Herb-Smoked Pork Chops

This is but one of three recipes in which I suggest that an herb be added to the grill to add a distinctive flavor, rather than wood chips. This dish is an unusual treat for both the host and the guests. It is very simple to prepare and involves very little grill time.

I am sure that you and your guests will appreciate the combined earthiness of the sage and the sweetness of the pork, which nicely compliment each other.

Wash and pat dry **3 pounds of center-cut pork chops.** Add **salt and pepper to taste** to both sides.

Place the chops on the grill over a direct fire and place **several sprigs of sage,** which have also been washed, on top of the chops and on the grill-top (do not place the sage on the coals). Cover with the lid. Grill for 10 minutes, turn over, and grill the other side for 8 minutes longer. Remove from the grill and serve immediately.

Fire: direct
Lid: covered
Wood Smoke: none
Total Grill Time: 18 minutes
Servings: 4

Smoked Pork Roast

This cut of pork is particularly well-suited to being smoked with apple wood chips. The recipe is highlighted by very simple preparation, easy grilling and wood smoking, beautiful presentation, and great taste. Because this cut of pork is lean, a baste is used to keep the meat moist and flavorful during grilling.

Purchase **4 pounds of boneless pork loin roast,** which has been tied by the butcher. Wash under cold water and pat dry.

Let sit at room temperature 1 hour before grilling. Place the roast in the middle of the grill over an indirect fire. Add apple wood chips to the coals and cover with the lid. Every 15 minutes brush the roast with the basting liquid (see below) and periodically turn the roast such that all sides are eventually basted. When the internal temperature of the roast reaches 170-175 degrees (approximately 1-3/4 hours), remove from the grill. Let sit at room temperature for 15 minutes, slice, and serve immediately.

Basting Liquid

Mix well the following ingredients: **1/2 cup of red wine vinegar, 1/4 cup of Dijon mustard, 1/4 cup of olive oil, 1/4 cup of soy sauce**, and **1 tablespoon of liquid hot pepper sauce** (optional).

Fire: indirect
Lid: covered
Wood Smoke: apple
Total Grill Time: 1-3/4 hours
Servings: 6 to 8

Grilled Pulled Pork Sandwiches

An unusual dish that is worth the time spent cooking the meat to create that great pulled pork taste. It is similar to the Grilled Pulled Beef recipe in the Beef Entree Section (see page 63) both in the way it is served as well as the amount Of preparation and grilling time.

This dish is rarely found outside of the Southeastern U.S. but will be a welcome treat, especially if served outside of its home territory.

Given that the pulled meat is served on a hamburger bun with a helping of barbecue sauce, its presentation invites an informal party atmosphere with side dishes of cole slaw and baked beans. In addition, you may grill the meat and pull it into shreds the day before your party and simply reheat the meat in the accompanying barbecue sauce the day of your get-together.

Purchase from your butcher **6 pounds of pork shoulder** (also called pork butt, but I don't know why since it really is from the shoulder section of the pig). Wash under cold water and pat dry. Add **salt and ground black pepper** to the top and sides of the meat. Refrigerate and remove to room temperature 1 hour before grilling.

Place the meat in the middle of the grill over an indirect fire. Cover with the lid and turn the top vent to the 3/4 open position to lower the temperature of the fire and slow the cooking process. When the internal temperature of the meat reaches 170 - 175 degrees (approximately 2-1/4 hours) remove from the grill. Let sit for 1 hour at room temperature and then tear the pork into shreds making sure to discard any fat and charred, hard-to-chew pieces. (At this point, you may refrigerate the shredded meat and reheat the following day.)

Place the meat (either just pulled from the shoulder or pulled the previous day and refrigerated) in the warm **barbecue sauce** (see below) that has been prepared in a saucepan (make sure to reserve 1 cup of the sauce to serve on the side with the sandwiches). Spoon the pork shreds onto **hamburger buns** and serve immediately.

As with the Grilled Pulled Beef recipe, store-bought barbecue sauces tend to smother the wonderful grilled taste of the pork you have worked so hard to create. The following 2 recipes are delicate enough to complement the pulled pork without overwhelming it. Each recipe requires few ingredients and each is easy to prepare. The first sauce recipe is the more common and has a tomato base. The second sauce recipe is more unusual in that it is mustard based. You may wish to offer your guests sandwiches containing both sauces and, if so, I would recommend halving the ingredients for each of the following sauce recipes.

Tomato-Based Barbecue Sauce

In a medium-size saucepan combine the following: **1/2 cup of finely chopped white onion** (1 medium size chopped onion), **1-1/2 cups of ketchup, 1/3 of cup of red wine vinegar, 1/2 cup of beer** (you can substitute 1/2 cup of water for the beer), **2 tablespoons of Worcestershire sauce,** and **2 teaspoons of liquid hot pepper sauce.** Bring to a boil, reduce heat and simmer for approximately 15 minutes, allowing the sauce to slightly thicken. Reserve 1 cup of the sauce and combine the pork shreds with the remaining sauce. Serve immediately with the reserved sauce on the side.

Mustard-Based Barbecue Sauce

In a medium-size saucepan combine the following: **1/2 cup of red wine vinegar, 1/2 cup of water, 3 tablespoons of olive oil, 1/4 cup of Dijon mustard, 1/4 cup of Worcestershire sauce**, and **2 teaspoons of liquid hot pepper sauce**. Bring to a boil, reduce heat and simmer for approximately 15 minutes, allowing the sauce to slightly thicken. Reserve 1 cup of the sauce and combine the pork shreds with the remaining sauce. Serve immediately with the reserved sauce on the side.

Fire: indirect
Lid: covered
Wood Smoke: none
Total Grill Time: 2 hours and 15 minutes
Servings: 14 to 16 sandwiches

Barbecue-Sauced Pork Ribs

These are probably what everyone has in mind when they think of barbecued food. The crispy outer meat surrounding the moist inside cannot be duplicated anywhere. Grillers in the South have perfected this dish and have elevated it to an art form, and for good reason. When cooked properly, the taste is mouth watering. Serving side dishes of baked beans and cole slaw will complete a meal that no one can resist.

Purchase from your butcher **6 pounds of baby back pork ribs** (which are much leaner than standard spareribs). Have the butcher split the ribs into 4 equal rack sections. Each section should be small enough to be maneuvered on the grill with ease while cooking. Rinse the ribs under cold water and pat dry. Add **salt and pepper to taste** to both sides.

Place the ribs, with the meaty side facing up, in the middle of the grill over a direct fire. Replace the lid and make sure to use the lid at all times to avoid flare-ups which may burn the meat. After 15 minutes, turn the ribs over, add a generous amount of **barbecue sauce** (see below) and grill for another 20 minutes making sure to turn the ribs and add barbecue sauce after 10 minutes. Check to see that the meat is done—the meat should be white to slightly pink. Remove from the grill and serve immediately with additional barbecue sauce on the side.

Unlike my recommendation against using store-bought barbecue sauces for Grilled Pulled Beef (see page 63) and Grilled Pulled Pork (see page 79), I do recommend these sauces for barbecue-sauced pork ribs. The sauce is added to the ribs while on the grill, unlike the pulled beef or pork recipes in which the sauce is added after the grilling is completed. In addition, barbecue-sauced pork ribs are intended to have a stronger flavored sauce to complement the neutral taste of this cut of pork; whereas, the sauce for pulled beef and pork sandwiches should be delicate, complimenting the grilled taste of the meat without overwhelming it.

Even though the store-bought sauces are very good, I have included the following barbecue sauce recipe, which is very quick and simple to prepare, and slightly spicy with a robust taste. If you are going to go through the effort of hosting a grilling party, why not spend a few minutes (you will most likely already have the ingredients in your pantry) adding that extra personal touch by creating your own barbecue sauce, which can even be made a day ahead? I am confident that you will find this sauce just as great tasting, if not more so, than any store-bought sauce.

Barbecue Sauce

In a medium-size saucepan add the following ingredients: **3/4 cup of finely-chopped white onion** (1 large chopped onion), **2 cups of ketchup, 3/8 cup of red wine vinegar, 1/2 cup of water, 1/4 cup of Worcestershire sauce, 3/8 cup of lightly packed brown sugar**, and **1 tablespoon of liquid hot pepper sauce.** Stir the ingredients and bring to a boil. Reduce the heat and let simmer for 15 minutes. Use immediately or, once cooled, pour into a container with a lid, cover tightly, and refrigerate.

Fire: direct
Lid: covered
Wood Smoke: none
Total Grill Time: 35 minutes
Servings: 4 to 6

Grilled Leg of Lamb

This recipe will produce wonderfully marinated lamb infused with red wine and rosemary, and with the texture of soft butter. There is no gamy taste—only delicate flavor and tender pieces of meat that your guests will most likely not encounter anywhere else.

Purchase **5 pounds of leg of lamb** which should be boned and butterflied by your butcher, yielding about **3 pounds of meat.**

In a nonreactive bowl combine the following for the marinade: **1/2 cup of dry red wine, 1/4 cup of olive oil, 1/4 cup of soy sauce, 2 teaspoons of dried rosemary, 1 teaspoon of ground black pepper**, and **2 teaspoons of minced garlic** (3 large garlic cloves). Pour the mixture over the lamb and marinate for at least 5 to 6 hours, preferably overnight.

One hour before grilling, remove from the refrigerator and let stand at room temperature. Remove the lamb from the marinade and discard the marinade. When ready to grill, position the lamb directly over the coals of an indirect fire for 3 minutes, turn over and grill for another 3 minutes to sear the meat. Move the lamb to the center of the grill, replace the lid, and grill for 15 minutes. Turn over and grill for another 15 minutes or until an instant meat thermometer reads 145 to 150 degrees. Remove immediately from the grill and let stand for 5 minutes. Cut into thin slices and serve immediately.

Fire: indirect
Lid: covered
Wood Smoke: none
Total Grill Time: 35 minutes
Servings: 6 to 8

Grilled Lamb Chops

This recipe is very different than the previous dish but still produces flavorful lamb with the same buttery texture. The preparation time is shorter than the previous lamb recipe since no marinade is used, and the grill time is also shorter.

Purchase from your butcher **3 pounds of center-cut lamb shoulder** which has been cut into 1/2 inch slices (about 12 chops).

Coat both sides of the lamb chops with **olive oil.** Add **3 tablespoons of finely chopped fresh rosemary** (taken partially from a whole sprig) to both sides of the chops. Add **salt and pepper to taste** to both sides.

Add the remaining unused sprig of rosemary to the coals and place the lamb on the grill over a direct fire. Cover with the lid. Grill for 8 minutes, turn over and grill for an additional 6 minutes. Remove from the grill and serve immediately.

Fire: direct
Lid: covered
Wood Smoke: none
Total Grill Time: 14 minutes
Servings: 6

Poultry

Poultry Entrees

This entree section has the distinction of representing two basic types of recipes: the most foolproof to prepare and grill—chicken breast, and the most impressive to grill and serve—smoked whole turkey.

The number of ways to grill chicken is limited only by your imagination. You can simply add salt and pepper to chicken breasts, place them directly over the coals, and allow the open flame to add its distinctive taste to the meat. You can use a sauce or a marinade for spiciness, or you can add flavor through wood smoking. Once grilled, you can slice the chicken and add to a Caesar salad, toss with pasta or rice, eat as a sandwich, or serve with numerous side dishes of your choice. No matter how it is grilled and served, you can be assured that it will be enjoyed by all.

Like hamburgers, chicken recipes can easily accommodate large parties; several chicken breasts can be grilled at once and in short order. As someone who has hosted many grilling parties during all the seasons of the year, chicken should always be considered when entertaining a large number of guests.

Turkey, on the other hand, should be prepared just one way—smoked over an indirect fire on Thanksgiving Day or Christmas. I can assure you that your family and guests will never forget its great taste and impressive appearance. One Christmas day I brought a smoked turkey, which I had spent the previous three hours smoking in my backyard, to a friend's house for dinner. The aroma from the still hot turkey, sensed by all at the party as soon as I walked in with it, added great excitement to an already special celebration. Needless to say, and to no one's surprise, the smoked turkey was the only dish of several served that evening that had no leftovers.

Poultry Recipes

Recipe	Preparation + Grill Time under 30 min.	Grill Time Under 20 min.	Loved by Children	Best with Wood Smoke
Smoked Turkey			X	X
Grilled Marinated Chicken		X	X	
Grilled Chicken Satay		X	X	
Grilled Chicken Tenders	X	X	X	
Barbecue-Sauced Chicken Tenders	X	X	X	
Smoked Chicken Tenders	X		X	X
Grilled Teriyaki Chicken Sandwiches		X	X	
Herb-Smoked Whole Chicken			?	X(herb)

Smoked Turkey

I know what you are thinking! "Grill a whole turkey on Thanksgiving or Christmas and perhaps destroy the entire holiday spirit with an undercooked/overcooked turkey? No way!!"

I must confess that I thought the same thing that very first time I considered grilling a whole turkey. On that fateful first Thanksgiving Day the moment I placed the turkey on the grill was the same moment my wife placed her turkey in the oven. That's how much confidence she had in my grilling abilities. However, I persevered but not without a significant degree of perspiration during the entire smoking process. Not only did the grilling and smoking with hickory chips work as expected and on time, but the family ate only my grilled turkey and didn't touch my wife's turkey (except to compare the differences in taste!).

If your spouse doesn't trust your grilling abilities either, or worse, you don't trust your own—then cook two turkeys. You can always eat the leftovers days later. I assure you that you and your turkey will be the talk of the party. Your family and guests will get into the grilling as much as you will. And, if your kitchen is equipped like mine with only one oven, your family will welcome your freeing-up the oven for the many side dishes and desserts.

This most recent Thanksgiving Day I grilled simultaneously a thirteen pound whole turkey, which was stuffed, and a six pound turkey breast. It took a total of three hours, about the same amount of time it would take to cook in an oven. Needless to say, it was a spectacular dinner and one of many in a long line of grilled turkeys served at my home on Thanksgiving Day.

Thirty minutes before grilling, place 50 charcoal briquettes in the chimney and light the newspaper. Then place 6 handfuls of hickory chips in water to soak. After 25 minutes, place half of the glowing briquettes on one side of the grill and the other half on the opposite side, with a drip pan placed in between the two piles. Place the **turkey, either unstuffed or stuffed** with your **favorite dressing** (and prepared identically to a traditional oven-roasted turkey), in the middle of the grill with a meat thermometer in place (you may want to wrap the exposed part of the meat thermometer with aluminum foil since it will become black from the smoke if left exposed). Add 1/2 of a handful of soaked and drained hickory chips to each of the mounds of charcoal on each side of the grill. Place the lid on the grill and make sure that the top and bottom vents are open.

Every 45 minutes add 4 or 5 briquettes to each side of the grill and every 30 minutes add 1/2 of a handful of soaked hickory chips to each side. After 2 hours of grilling, begin to check the internal meat temperature periodically. Remove the turkey from the grill once it has reached an internal temperature of 175 to 180 degrees. If the turkey is cooking faster than expected, you can slow down the process by closing partially or completely the top vent. The turkey will cook faster if: the outside air temperature is warm (I cooked my turkey when the outside temperature was 40 degrees); the total turkey weight on the grill is less than 18 to 20 pounds; and the turkey is unstuffed.

You may also wish to reheat **extra stuffing** by transferring it to a disposable aluminum pan and placing the pan on the grill 30 minutes before the turkey is ready to be removed.

Finally, let the turkey sit for 15 minutes before you are ready to carve so it retains its natural juices. Then carve, serve, and enjoy your great tasting turkey dinner.

I am confident that you will have a lot of fun grilling the turkey. It will be a great conversation piece, taste much better than its oven-baked brother, and your family and guests will be the lucky participants in a never-to-be-forgotten Thanksgiving celebration.

Fire: indirect
Lid: covered
Wood Smoke: hickory
Total Grill Time: 3 to 3-1/2 hrs. for a 13 pound stuffed turkey and 6 pound turkey breast
Servings: More than you will need unless you are serving an army

Grilled Marinated Chicken

This is my favorite chicken dish. As with Grilled Marinated Shrimp (see page 108), it is one of the best examples of minimalist grilling: it has few ingredients, little preparation effort, very little grill time, and a great taste.

Rinse **1-1/2 pounds of chicken breast, skinless and boneless,** under cold water and pat dry. Separate into 4 equal pieces.

For the marinade, mix together the following ingredients in a nonreactive bowl: **1-1/2 tablespoons of olive oil, 3 tablespoons of lemon juice (juice of 1 large lemon), 1 tablespoon of Dijon mustard, 3 tablespoons of white wine Worcestershire sauce, 1 teaspoon of minced garlic** (1 large garlic clove), and **2 teaspoons of liquid hot pepper sauce.** Place the chicken in the marinade, cover, and refrigerate for 3 to 4 hours.

One-half hour before grilling, remove from the refrigerator and let stand at room temperature. Remove the chicken from the marinade and discard the marinade. Place the chicken on the grill over a direct fire for 7 to 8 minutes. Turn and grill for another 5 to 6 minutes. Remove from the grill and serve immediately.

Fire: direct
Lid: uncovered
Wood Smoke: none
Total Grill Time: 12 to 14 minutes
Servings: 4

Grilled Chicken Satay

A very simple dish to prepare and a very exotic treat for your guests. The ingredients are a lot less than anyone would imagine and the grill time is very short.

If you like, cut the chicken into small pieces after grilling and serve as an appetizer.

Rinse **1-1/2 pounds of chicken breasts, skinless and boneless,** under cold water and pat dry. Separate into 4 equal pieces.

Whisk together the following ingredients in a non-reactive bowl: **3 tablespoons of creamy peanut butter, 1/4 cup of lime juice, 1/4 cup of soy sauce, 2 teaspoons of minced garlic** (3 large garlic cloves), and **2 teaspoons of hot pepper sauce.** Place the chicken in the marinade making sure to coat all sides with the marinade. Cover and refrigerate for up to 3-4 hours.

One-half hour before grilling, remove from the refrigerator and let stand at room temperature. Remove the chicken from the marinade and discard the marinade. Place the chicken on the grill over a direct fire, and grill for 7 to 8 minutes. Turn and grill for another 5 to 6 minutes. Remove from the grill and serve immediately.

Fire: direct
Lid: uncovered
Wood Smoke: none
Total Grill Time: 12 to 14 minutes
Servings: 4

Grilled Chicken Tenders

One of the easiest to prepare, most versatile, and most universally liked dishes. These pieces of white-meat chicken can be grilled and served as a main course or sliced and added to pasta, rice, or salad greens.

Rinse **1-1/2 pounds of chicken breasts, skinless and boneless,** under cold water and pat dry. Separate into 4 equal pieces. Add **salt and pepper to taste.**

Place the chicken over a direct fire and grill for 7 minutes. Turn over and grill for another 5 minutes. Remove the chicken from the grill and serve whole or sliced with rice, pasta, or salad greens.

To add an exotic taste to this entree, the **Black Bean and Lime Salsa** found in the recipe for Grilled Swordfish (see page 105) is an excellent accompaniment to this dish.

Fire: direct
Lid: uncovered
Wood Smoke: none
Total Grill Time: 12 minutes
Servings: 4

Barbecue-Sauced Chicken Tenders

This is how chicken was intended to be served: grilled over hot coals with a coat of simple-to-prepare barbecue sauce brushed on for additional spicy flavor.

Rinse **1-1/2 pounds of chicken breasts, skinless and boneless,** under cold water and pat dry. Separate into 4 equal pieces.

Place the chicken on the grill over a direct fire for 12 to 15 minutes making sure to turn the chicken and brush on a generous amount of **barbecue sauce** (see below) every 4 to 5 minutes. Remove and serve immediately.

I have included the following barbecue sauce recipe which is very quick and simple to prepare. I am confident that you will find this sauce just as great tasting, if not more so, than any store-bought sauce.

Barbecue Sauce

In a medium-size pot add the following ingredients: **1/2 cup of finely-chopped white onion** (one medium size onion), **1 cup of ketchup, 1/4 cup of red wine vinegar, 1/4 cup of water, 2 tablespoons of Worcestershire sauce, 3 tablespoons of brown sugar**, and **2 teaspoons of liquid hot pepper sauce.** Stir the ingredients and bring to a boil. Reduce the heat and let simmer for 15 minutes. Use immediately or, once cooled, pour into a container with a lid, cover tightly, and refrigerate.

Fire: direct
Lid: uncovered
Wood Smoke: none
Total Grill Time: 12 to 15 minutes
Servings: 4

Smoked Chicken Tenders

A very simple entree that requires nothing more than salt and pepper to taste and wood chips for smoke. Of course, the taste is very different from grilled (unsmoked) chicken. Relative to other wood-smoked entrees, the smoking time is unusually short.

Rinse **1-1/2 pounds of chicken breasts, skinless and boneless,** under cold water and pat dry. Separate into 4 equal pieces. Add **salt and pepper to taste.**

Place the chicken over an indirect fire to which you've added soaked and drained wood chips. Replace the lid and smoke for 15 minutes. Turn and smoke for another 8 to 10 minutes. Remove from the grill and serve immediately.

Fire: indirect
Lid: covered
Wood Smoke: hickory or mesquite
Total Grill Time: 23 to 25 minutes
Servings: 4

Grilled Teriyaki Chicken Sandwiches

Unlike its sandwich cousins—Grilled Pulled Beef (see page 63) and Grilled Pulled Pork (see page 79), this is a very quick and easy recipe. The marinade time is only two hours, and the preparation and grill times are very short. Also, the taste is unusual, especially for a sandwich. Make sure to have lettuce and tomatoes available to accompany the chicken.

Rinse **1-1/2 pounds of chicken breasts, skinless and boneless,** under cold water and pat dry. Separate into 4 or more equal pieces.

In a bowl, combine: **1/2 cup of soy sauce, 1/4 cup of olive oil, 1/4 cup of red wine vinegar, 1 teaspoon of minced garlic** (1 large garlic clove), **1 teaspoon of liquid hot pepper sauce,** and **1/2 teaspoon of ground black pepper.** Place the chicken in the marinade, cover, and refrigerate for 3 to 4 hours.

One-half hour before grilling, remove from the refrigerator and let stand at room temperature. Remove the chicken from the marinade and discard the marinade. Place the chicken on the grill over a direct fire, and grill for 7 to 8 minutes. Turn and grill for another 3 to 4 minutes. Remove immediately from the grill and serve on **hamburger buns.** Have **lettuce and tomato** available for your guests to garnish their sandwiches.

Fire: direct
Lid: uncovered
Wood Smoke: none
Total Grill Time: 10 to 12 minutes
Servings: 4

Herb-Smoked Whole Chicken

This very simple-to-prepare recipe will produce a succulent whole grilled chicken that is slightly flavored throughout with the scent of rosemary. The meat will remain moist and tender due to the slow grilling process, identical to that for smoked turkey. I am confident that your guests will rarely have encountered, if ever, such an unusual chicken dish.

Purchase a **3 to 3-1/2 pound whole chicken.** Remove and discard the neck and any giblets. Rinse both the cavity and the outside of the chicken with cold water and pat dry. Rub **salt and ground black pepper** in the cavity and outside section. Place **6 sprigs of fresh rosemary** and **1 lemon** (which has been sliced into 4 wedges) into the cavity of the chicken.

Place the chicken over an indirect fire, replace the lid, and grill until the internal temperature reaches 180 to 185 degrees (approximately 1-1/4 to 1-1/2 hours). Remove the chicken from the grill and discard the lemon wedges and sprigs of rosemary. Let the chicken sit for 5 minutes before carving so that it retains its natural juices. Carve and serve immediately.

Fire: indirect
Lid: covered
Wood Smoke: none
Total Grill Time: 1-1/4 to 1-1/2 hours
Servings: 4

Fish

Fish Entrees

It goes without saying that fish, almost any kind of fish, tastes best when grilled over a hot fire. The best evidence of this are those individuals, like my children and I, who will eat swordfish, salmon, and most other types of fish only if they have been grilled. The direct heat and smoke alter the tastes and textures to a greater extent than other types of cooking, and the fish very nicely loses that "fishy taste."

Like the taste, the appearance of grilled fish is also unique. The intense grill marks on swordfish and salmon steaks, the slightly charred exterior of grilled shrimp, and the dark red color of smoked salmon add to the enjoyment of any fish meal. In fact, I think that the grilling and smoking of fish adds more to its taste and appearance than the grilling and smoking of beef, lamb, and chicken.

For those watching their weight or concerned about their health, there are very few entrees, cooked in any fashion, that contain as little fat as the following recipes (and very few that taste so good!).

One final benefit of grilling fish is the very short grill time. All of the entrees, excluding the ones for smoked salmon, require between eight and twenty minutes for proper grilling. As entrees go, this is very short. By the way, do not let the longer cooking time for the Smoked Salmon and Smoked Whitefish entrees deter you from preparing them: the taste and appearance are worth the wait, and the effort is minimal.

I am sure that once you try a few of these recipes you will agree that grilling over a charcoal fire will turn almost anyone into a fish lover, and turn the fish lover into someone who must own a charcoal grill.

Fish Recipes

Recipe	Preparation + Grill Time under 30 min.	Grill Time Under 20 min.	Loved by Children	Best with Wood Smoke
Grilled Swordfish	X	X	?	
Grilled Shrimp	X	X	X	?
Grilled Marinated Shrimp		X	X	
Grilled Shrimp Satay		X	X	
Grilled Salmon	X	X	?	
Grilled Marinated Salmon		X	?	
Smoked Salmon			?	X
Grilled Tuna Filet	X	X		
Grilled Scallops with Pesto Sauce		X		
Smoked Whitefish			?	X

Grilled Swordfish

My favorite fish entree to grill. The taste is that of neither fish nor meat but a completely new taste experience. Once grilled, you can add either a squeeze of lemon or a black bean and lime salsa, both of which enhance the flavor without smothering it.

This dish, when paired with the right appetizer and the right wine, will turn any gathering into the most elegant and unique of occasions.

Purchase **1-1/2 pounds of fresh swordfish and have the fish cut into 1/2 to 3/4 inch thick slices.** Try not to use slices thicker than 3/4 inch as the inside may not cook as well as expected, nor accept cuts much less than 1/2 inch thick as the inside may overcook and become tough. Rinse the raw fish under cold water, pat dry, and add **salt and pepper to taste.**

Place the swordfish on the grill over a direct fire. After 7 minutes turn the fish sideways 90 degrees and continue grilling for another 3 minutes. Turn over and cook for an additional 5 to 7 minutes.

Remove from the grill and serve immediately with the cross-hatched side facing up. Garnish with a **slice of lemon** or the following **Black Bean and Lime Salsa.** Best served with your favorite rice.

Fire: direct
Lid: uncovered
Wood Smoke: none
Total Grill Time: 15 to 17 minutes
Servings: 4

Black Bean and Lime Salsa

In a large bowl combine the following: **1 can of cooked black beans (16 ounces),** which has been drained and the beans rinsed under cold water, **1/2 cup of chopped white onion** (1 medium onion), **1 jalapeño pepper,** which has been seeded and chopped (optional), **3 tablespoons of minced cilantro, 2 teaspoons of minced garlic** (3 large garlic cloves), **1 teaspoon of prepared mustard**, and **1/3 cup of lime juice.** Mix well and add **salt and pepper to taste.**

Grilled Shrimp

One of the best pasta dishes you will ever taste is my grilled shrimp served over linguine with sliced Grilled Portobello Mushrooms. The earthiness of the mushrooms combined with the crunchy shrimp and soft linguine make for a very memorable meal.

This is one of the few dishes that my finicky nine year old son will eat. My daughter of eleven years, on the other hand, will eat anything. When my son first saw the grilled shrimp they looked too appetizing to pass up, so he tried one. Guess what? He liked it and ate several more. He won't eat just any shrimp dish, like traditional shrimp cocktail—only my grilled shrimp. If you have young children (or old children for that matter) who don't like anything except hot dogs and hamburgers, give this dish a try. I hope you have a similar experience.

Purchase **1-1/2 pounds of large shrimp** and have them shelled, deveined, and the heads removed. Rinse them under cold water and pat dry.

Just before you grill the shrimp, make sure to grill the **portobello mushrooms** (see page 28). Slice the grilled mushrooms and add to the linguine at the same time that you add the shrimp.

Thread the shrimp onto metal or bamboo skewers and place over a direct fire. Grill for 4 minutes and turn for another 3 minutes. Make sure to remove from the fire as soon as they have turned from glossy to opaque. If you prefer, slice in half and add to **hot linguine**, or serve them separately.

Fire: direct
Lid: uncovered
Wood Smoke: hickory or mesquite (optional)
Total Grill Time: 7 minutes
Servings: 6

Grilled Marinated Shrimp

This is my favorite shrimp dish. As with Grilled Marinated Chicken (see page 94), this is one of the best examples of minimalist grilling: it has few ingredients, little preparation effort, very short grill time, and a great taste.

Purchase **1-1/2 pounds of large shrimp** that have been deveined and the heads and shells removed. Rinse the shrimp under cold water and pat dry.

For the marinade, mix together the following ingredients in a nonreactive bowl: **2 tablespoons of olive oil, 3 tablespoons of lemon juice** (juice of 1 large lemon), **1 tablespoon of Dijon mustard, 3 tablespoons of white wine Worcestershire sauce, 1 teaspoon of minced garlic** (1 large garlic clove), and **2 teaspoons of liquid hot pepper sauce.** Add the shrimp to the marinade, cover, and refrigerate for up to 2 hours.

One-half hour before grilling, remove the bowl from the refrigerator and let stand at room temperature. Remove the shrimp from the marinade and discard the marinade. Thread the shrimp on metal or bamboo skewers and place them over a direct fire for 4 minutes. Turn and grill for another 3 minutes. Make sure to remove the shrimp from the fire as soon as they have turned from glossy to opaque. Remove from the grill and serve immediately.

Fire: direct
Lid: uncovered
Wood Smoke: none
Total Grill Time: 7 minutes
Servings: 6

Grilled Shrimp Satay

Like the Grilled Chicken Satay recipe (see page 95), this is a very simple dish to prepare and a very exotic treat for your guests. While the preparation requires the shrimp to be placed in a marinade for several hours, the grill time is very short.

Purchase **1-1/2 pounds of large shrimp** that have been deveined and the heads and shells removed. Rinse the shrimp in cold water and pat dry.

Mix together the following ingredients in a nonreactive bowl: **3 tablespoons of creamy peanut butter, 1/4 cup of lime juice, 1/4 cup of soy sauce, 1 tablespoon of minced garlic** (3 large garlic cloves), and **2 teaspoons of liquid hot pepper sauce.** Place the shrimp in the marinade, cover, and refrigerate for up to 2 hours.

One-half hour before grilling, remove the bowl from the refrigerator and let stand at room temperature. Remove the shrimp from the marinade and discard the marinade. Thread the shrimp onto skewers and place them on the grill over a direct fire. Grill the shrimp for 4 minutes, turn over and grill for another 3 minutes. Remove from the grill and serve.

Fire: direct
Lid: uncovered
Wood Smoke: none
Total Grill Time: 7 minutes
Servings: 6

Grilled Salmon

This is my wife's favorite fish entree, after grilled swordfish, because of the unique taste imparted by grilling. Due to salmon's high fat content you can cook it over a direct fire to char the outside while the inside meat remains moist.

Purchase from your local fish market **salmon steaks that are 1/2 to 3/4 inches thick or a salmon filet that is 1 to 1-1/2 inches thick.** One salmon steak will provide 1 serving and 1 filet will yield 1 or 2 servings, depending upon the size of the filet. Rinse under cold water and pat dry. **Add salt and pepper to taste.**

Place the salmon on the grill over a direct fire and grill for 5 to 7 minutes. Turn over and grill for an another 5 minutes. Remove from the grill and serve immediately.

Fire: direct
Lid: uncovered
Wood Smoke: none
Total Grill Time: 10 to 12 minutes
Servings: 1 salmon steak per person and 1 salmon filet for 1 to 2 people

Grilled Marinated Salmon

This great tasting recipe is simple to prepare and the marinade is mild enough to allow the natural flavor of the salmon to be enjoyed by everyone.

Purchase from your local fish market **1-1/2 pounds of salmon filet**, with the filet being 1 to 1-1/2 inches thick. Wash under cold water and pat dry.

For the marinade, mix together the following ingredients: **3/4 cup of soy sauce, 1/2 cup of brown sugar, 2 tablespoons of olive oil, 1 teaspoon of minced garlic** (1 clove of garlic), and **1/2 teaspoon of dried ginger.** Place the salmon in the marinade, cover, and refrigerate for up to 2 hours.

One-half hour before grilling, remove from the refrigerator and let stand at room temperature. Remove the salmon from the marinade and discard the marinade. Place the salmon on the grill, over a direct fire, and grill for 10 minutes. Turn over and grill for another 7 to 8 minutes. Remove from the grill and serve immediately.

Fire: direct
Lid: uncovered
Wood Smoke: none
Total Grill Time: 17 to 18 minutes
Servings: 4

Smoked Salmon

This is one of the most beautiful dishes in this handbook as well as one of the best tasting. The wood smoke transforms the pink meat of the salmon to a dark red color and complements the taste of the fish with a mild earth flavor.

The soaking of the fish in a sugar and salt water bath before grilling firms up the flesh as does the slow indirect smoking. While the preparation time is long, the grilling time is not extensive, and the simplicity of the ingredients combined with the slow cooking creates a complex taste that can't be matched.

Purchase **1-1/2 pounds of salmon filet** with the skin still on one side. Rinse the fish in cold water and place in a nonreactive dish with **2 quarts of cold water**, **1/2 cup of sugar,** and **1/4 cup of coarse salt.** Cover and refrigerate for a least 6 hours or overnight.

Just before grilling, remove the salmon from the water bath, rinse under cold water, and pat dry. Discard the water bath. Place the salmon in the middle of the grill over an indirect fire to which you've added hickory wood chips. Replace the lid and smoke for 1 to 1-1/4 hours. The salmon will become a dark red color and will be fully cooked when it is firm to the touch and beginning to flake. Remove from the grill and serve immediately.

Fire: indirect
Lid: covered
Wood Smoke: hickory
Total Grill Time: 1 to 1-1/4 hours
Servings: 4

Grilled Tuna Filet

The delicate nature of this fish, as well as its dark dense meat, require careful grilling so that the outside has a very light charring and the inside is not overcooked. The final result is a great tasting fish entree.

Purchase **tuna filets** that are about 3/4 inch thick and weigh 6 to 8 ounces each. Each filet will serve 1 person. Coat the fish on both sides with **olive oil** and add **salt and pepper to taste.**

Place the tuna on the grill over a direct fire for 4 to 5 minutes. Turn over and cook for an additional 3 minutes. Remove and serve immediately.

Fire: direct
Lid: uncovered
Wood Smoke: none
Total Grill Time: 7 to 8 minutes
Servings: 1 tuna filet per person

Grilled Scallops with Pesto Sauce

The scallops, along with mushrooms, are marinated in the pesto sauce, skewered, and then grilled. When served over rice or pasta, you'll create an enticing light meal highlighting the unique taste and delicate texture of the shellfish.

Rinse under cold water **1 pound of sea scallops (about 20 scallops)** and cut each in half. Also rinse **20 small mushrooms** under cold water. Pat dry the scallops and the mushrooms.

For the sauce, place **4 teaspoons of minced garlic** (6 garlic cloves) and **3 cups of basil leaves** (that have been rinsed and patted dry) in a food processor. With the motor running, drizzle in **1/2 cup of olive oil.** Transfer the mixture to a bowl and add **1 teaspoon of salt** and **1 teaspoon of ground black pepper.** Place the scallops and the mushrooms in the sauce, cover, and refrigerate for 1 to 2 hours.

One-half hour before you are ready to grill, remove from the refrigerator, discard the sauce, and thread the scallops onto skewers adding 2 halves of a sea scallop for each mushroom. Place the skewers on the grill, directly over the coals, and grill for 8 minutes. Turn over and grill for another 5 to 7 minutes. Remove from the grill and serve immediately.

Fire: direct
Lid: uncovered
Wood Smoke: none
Total Grill Time: 13 to 15 minutes
Servings: 4

Smoked Whitefish

Like its cousin, Smoked Trout (see page 27), this dish is very simple to prepare and elegant but seldom encountered. Because it has a sweeter and lighter taste than Smoked Trout, it is best enjoyed as an entree rather than an appetizer.

Purchase **one 5 pound, whole, fresh Lake Superior Whitefish** from your local fish store. Have the head and scales removed and the fish deboned and sliced open. It should weigh about 3 pounds after it has been cleaned.

Add the fish to a shallow pan with **2 quarts of cold water** and **1/4 cup of coarse salt**. Cover and place in the refrigerator for 2 to 4 hours.

When you are ready to grill, remove the fish from the salt water, rinse under cold water, and pat dry. Apply a **light coat of olive oil** to the skin side of the fish so that it will not stick to the grill during cooking. **Add pepper to taste** to the nonskin side of the fish.

Place the whitefish, skin side down, in the middle of an indirect fire. Add hickory wood chips to the coals and cover with the lid. Let it cook for 35 to 40 minutes, or until the flesh of the fish begins to pull away from the skin.

Remove from the grill and, with a sharp knife, cut the meat away from the skin. Divide into four sections and serve immediately.

Fire: indirect
Lid: covered
Wood Smoke: hickory
Total Grill Time: 35 to 40 minutes
Servings: 4 to 6

Accompaniments

Accompaniments

Side dishes such as salads, baked beans, and cole slaw are often considered last when planning a grilling party, if they are considered at all. Often, so much effort is put into preparing the appetizers and the entrees that no time or energy is left to consider the accompaniments. This is unfortunate since no grilling is necessary and only a small amount of preparation is needed before the guests arrive.

Accompaniments should always be considered with care when matching them with the entree. The accompaniment selected should be complementary to the entrees by adding balance and contrasting textures. I am sure you will agree that adding side dishes of baked beans and cole slaw to a serving of barbecue-sauced pork ribs elevates an already tasty entree to a truly memorable meal for all involved.

All of the following side dishes have little to do with grilling except that they are often served alongside grilled foods. All but one, baked beans, are served cool or at room temperature, making for one less complication when grilling the rest of the meal. In addition, all of these accompaniments can be prepared in under 30 minutes. I hope that you will discover many others that are just as rewarding, if not more so, than these few simple recipes.

Salad with Vinaigrette Dressing

While the number of salads you can serve are too numerous to mention, my wife makes this slightly sweet tasting salad that is a perfect accompaniment to grilled foods, especially those that are spicy. The salad greens are basic lettuce leaves, and the dressing is a snap to make and a treat to eat.

This recipe will serve 8

Separate **2 heads of your favorite lettuce** and place in a bowl.

In a blender combine the following: **1/3 cup of white balsamic vinegar (or regular balsamic vinegar), 1/2 cup sugar, 1 cup olive oil, 1 teaspoon of salt, 1/4 cup of chopped white onion** (1/2 of a chopped onion), **1 teaspoon of Dijon mustard,** and **2 tablespoons of water**. Combine all ingredients in a blender and blend until smooth. Refrigerate until ready to use. Toss with salad just before serving.

Tomatoes with Mozzarella and Onions

This dish is very easy to prepare since you need only to slice tomatoes, cheese, and onions before serving. Despite the ease of preparation, the taste is cool and crisp, nicely complementing any grilled meal.

This recipe will serve 6

Slice **3 red tomatoes, 1 large white onion, and 1 pound of mozzarella cheese.** Arrange 3 slices of tomato on a small plate, add 3 slices of the cheese, and top with 2 to 3 slices of the onion. Add **salt and pepper to taste** (as an option drizzle over the top a small amount of **olive oil and balsamic vinegar).** Serve immediately.

Pasta Salad

This side dish is simple to make and a real treat for children and adults alike. The taste is light and refreshing and thus can accompany just about any entree.

This recipe will serve 6 to 8

In a saucepan heat **1/4 cup of olive oil** to a medium-high temperature and add the following: **2 cups of broccoli florets, 1/3 cup of chopped scallions (about 1 bunch scallions), 1/2 teaspoon of minced garlic** (1 clove of garlic), and **1/2 teaspoon of salt.** Heat and stir until broccoli has cooked, about 4 minutes. Remove the saucepan from the heat and toss with **pasta (8 ounces of dried pasta** that has been cooked and drained) and **1/2 cup of grated Parmesan cheese.** Garnish with **several cherry tomatoes** (optional). Chill and serve.

Slightly Spicy Baked Beans

You can't serve grilled meat, especially pork, at an informal party without serving baked beans. The sweetness of the sauce and the slight crunchiness of the beans add a wonderful dimension to any grilled meal. There is no grilling time and as baked bean dishes go, this one is ready in very short order.

This recipe will serve 4 to 6

Place the following ingredients in a pot: **2 cans (12 ounces per can) of vegetarian baked beans** (no meat added) that have been drained, **1/4 cup of maple syrup, 1/4 cup of ketchup, 1/4 cup of brown sugar, 1 teaspoon of liquid hot pepper sauce, 2 teaspoons of Worcestershire sauce**, and **salt and pepper to taste.**

Mix the ingredients together and heat until the beans begin to simmer, then reduce the heat to low and cook uncovered for 20 minutes. Serve immediately.

Cole Slaw

While rice and pasta are great to serve with grilled food, there is something comforting about the informal look and taste of cole slaw. There is no grilling involved and the preparation time is short. This recipe has a garden fresh taste and uses very little mayonnaise.

This recipe will serve 8 to 10

Shred **1 green cabbage**, to yield 12 to 14 cups, and mix in **2 tablespoons of sugar** and **1 tablespoon of salt.** Let stand for 30 minutes until the cabbage has wilted slightly. Pour out the liquid that forms. Mix in **3 large peeled carrots** which have been grated.

In a separate bowl combine **1/3 cup of mayonnaise** and **3 tablespoons of white balsamic vinegar.** (This will create a cole slaw with just a hint of mayonnaise. Should you prefer more of a mayonnaise taste, then use a mixture of **1/2 cup of mayonnaise** and **1/4 cup of white balsamic vinegar.**) Pour the mixture over the cabbage and carrot mixture. Mix well and refrigerate. Serve when cool.

Health Salad

This second version of cole slaw is as fresh-tasting as the first with the same short amount of preparation time. The difference is that this recipe is even lower in calories, since it contains no mayonnaise.

This recipe will serve 8 to 10

Shred **1 green cabbage,** to yield 12 to 14 cups, and mix in **2 tablespoons of sugar** and **1 tablespoon of salt.** Let stand 30 minutes until the cabbage has wilted slightly. Pour out the liquid that forms. Mix in **3 large peeled carrots** that have been grated, **3/4 cup of chopped red onion** (1 large chopped onion), and **1/3 cup of white balsamic vinegar.** Add **pepper to taste.** Mix well and refrigerate. Serve when cool.

Cold Sesame Noodles

This very tasty but unusual dish is one of the first to be finished when I serve it to my guests. There is no grilling, the preparation time is short, and the dish need not be kept heated. What more can you ask for!

This recipe will serve 6 to 8

Place in boiling water **one package (16 ounces) of dried spaghetti or linguine noodles** and cook until al dente. Immediately remove from heat and rinse under cold water to stop the cooking process. Mix in 1 **tablespoon of olive oil.** Let sit at room temperature.

In a nonreactive bowl mix the following: **3 tablespoons of sesame oil, 3 tablespoons of soy sauce, 1 teaspoon of balsamic vinegar, 2 tablespoons of sugar**, and **1/2 cup of chopped scallions** (about one bunch of scallions). When ready to serve, coat the noodles with the mixture and serve immediately.

Desserts

Desserts

The list of desserts that can be served to compliment a grilled meal is far too lengthy to include in this handbook. Nonetheless, the more common desserts found at a typical backyard grill-out include: brownies, cookies, pies, fresh fruit, and, of course, ice cream. A grilled dessert, on the other hand, is the furthest from anyone's mind when planning a grilling party. This is unfortunate—a grilled dessert will add further mystery to your party. Your guests will stare in disbelief when they see that dessert (not just roasted marshmallows) can be grilled.

The following recipes center on grilling fruit. These recipes require very little preparation time and just a few minutes of grill time, and use the still hot coals left over from grilling the entree. The remaining nonfruit recipes require no preparation and just a few minutes of grilling. In addition to little preparation effort and just a few minutes of grill time, all of these desserts have the taste and texture of caramelized sugar: the heating of the natural and added sugars produce that great caramel taste seldom encountered anywhere.

I am confident you will find the following recipes simple to prepare and quick to grill: that your guests will be enchanted by the idea of a grilled dessert; and that everyone will be delighted by the unique grilled taste presented at the end of what I am sure will be a memorable meal for all.

Desserts

Recipe	Preparation + Grill Time under 30 min.	Grill Time Under 20 min.	Loved by Children	Best with Wood Smoke
Grilled Bananas	X	X	X	
Grilled Apples	X	X	X	
Grilled Pineapples	X	X	X	
Grilled Pears	X	X	X	
Grilled Pound Cake	X	X	X	
Roasted Marshmallows	X	X	X	

Grilled Bananas

Brownies, cookies, cakes, ice cream, and fresh fruit are wonderful desserts for a grilling party, especially if your guests request that they bring something for the event; however, the following dessert is such an unusual treat that I guarantee it will be one of the many highlights of your party. I think that a scoop of vanilla ice cream is a great addition to this unique dessert.

Mix the following ingredients in a bowl: **1/2 cup of brown sugar, 1/4 cup of granulated sugar, 2 teaspoons of ground cinnamon,** and **2 teaspoons of nutmeg.**

Purchase **6 bananas that are yellow with a green tip.** Do not use over-ripe bananas or bananas that are green. Slice open the peel only on the inside curved section of each banana and loosen the banana from its peel. Spread the mixture between the banana and the peel, close the peel, and add **1 tablespoon of butter,** broken into several small pieces, where the peel was sliced open. As an option, drizzle **1 teaspoon of rum** over the length of the split banana.

Place the bananas on a sheet of aluminum foil, place the foil sheet on the grill directly over the coals of a direct or indirect fire, and cover with the lid. Grill for 10 minutes. Remove and serve with the peel (add a **scoop of vanilla ice cream,** as an option).

Fire: direct or indirect, whichever is used for the entree
Lid: covered
Wood Smoke: none
Total Grill Time: 10 minutes
Servings: 6

Grilled Apples

This recipe is just as unusual and just as tasty as the previous one. And like the previous recipe, I would recommend that a scoop of vanilla ice cream accompany this dessert.

Slice **3 red apples** and place the slices of each apple onto a sheet of aluminum foil. Mix the following ingredients in a bowl: **1/3 cup of brown sugar, 1 teaspoon of ground cinnamon**, and **1 teaspoon of nutmeg.** Sprinkle the mixture over the apple slices and add **1/2 tablespoon of butter** to each slice, broken into several small pieces.

Place the apple slices on a sheet of aluminum foil, place the foil sheet directly over the coals of a direct or indirect fire, and cover with the lid. Grill for 8 minutes. Remove from the grill, and, as an option, serve with a scoop of **vanilla ice cream.**

Fire: direct or indirect, whichever is used for the entree
Lid: covered
Wood Smoke: none
Total Grill Time: 8 minutes
Servings: 6

Grilled Pineapples

This very simple to prepare dessert becomes a refreshing one to enjoy as the outside of each pineapple ring becomes caramelized by the heating of the natural sugars. Only grill fresh pineapple; the canned version does not taste nearly as good since it is packaged in a sugary syrup.

For each **4 slices of fresh pineapple** (each slice should be about 1/2 to 3/4 inch thick), mix in a bowl: **1/3 cup of brown sugar, 2 teaspoons of water**, and **2 teaspoons of rum** (you may substitute additional water for the rum). Spread the mixture over each side of the pineapple slices.

Place the pineapples on the grill, directly over the coals of a direct or indirect fire, and cover with the lid. Grill for 4 minutes, turn over and grill for another 4 minutes. Remove from the grill, and, as an option, serve with a **scoop of vanilla ice cream.**

Fire: direct or indirect, whichever is used for the entree
Lid: covered
Wood Smoke: none
Total Grill Time: 8 minutes
Servings: 4

Grilled Pears

This recipe is similar to the previous one for Grilled Pineapples except that it is sweeter and less tart. Since the sugar coating that is added to the pears is the same as that used for the grilled pineapples recipe, consider serving a combination of the two; the tastes and textures will complement each other. And, of course, use only fresh pears since, like the pineapple recipe, the canned version does not taste nearly as good since the pears are packaged in a sugary syrup.

For each **4 fresh pear halves** (which have been seeded), mix the following: **1/3 cup of brown sugar, 2 teaspoons of water,** and **2 teaspoons of rum** (you may substitute water for the rum). Spread the mixture over the flat side of each pear.

Place the pears on the grill, directly over the coals of a direct or indirect fire, and cover with the lid. Grill for 4 minutes, turn over and grill for another 4 minutes. Remove from the grill, and, as an option, serve with a **scoop of vanilla ice cream.**

Fire: direct or indirect, whichever is used for the entree
Lid: covered
Wood Smoke: none
Total Grill Time: 8 minutes
Servings: 4

Grilled Pound Cake

An unusual dessert and one of a few that is tailor-made for the grill. The sugar in the cake becomes caramelized by the fire creating an unusual treat especially when accompanied by fresh fruit like strawberries or blueberries. There is practically no preparation time and the grill time is very short.

Cut the **pound cake** (either store-bought or homemade) into 1 inch slices and place on the grill directly over the coals. Grill for 3 minutes and turn and grill for another 3 minutes. Remove and serve immediately with your **favorite fruit.** As an option add **whipped cream.**

Fire: direct or indirect, whichever is used for the entree
Lid: uncovered
Wood Smoke: none
Total Grill Time: 6 minutes
Servings: 1 per slice of pound cake

Roasted Marshmallows

*It couldn't be any simpler—***marshmallows** *threaded on a stick.*

A crowd pleaser for the kids and something for them to look forward to while you are grilling the dinner.

Fire: direct or indirect, whichever is used for the entree
Lid: uncovered
Wood Smoke: none
Total Grill Time: na
Servings: 1 bag should feed 6 children, or 6 adults behaving like children

Beverages

Beverages

Just about any beverage goes well with grilled food. On the non-alcoholic side are lemonades, iced teas, and sodas. On the alcoholic side are beers, wines, daiquiris, margaritas, and wine-based drinks.

If your backyard party is informal, consider serving a selection of your favorite beers and sodas since neither requires preparation and your guests can choose what to drink.

A more formal party lends itself to serving wines. Both red and white wines go well with grilled food. Just keep in mind that a spicy or wood-smoked meal should be complemented by a full-bodied wine. I tend to like dry white wines like Chenin Blanc or Chardonnay. Of the reds, I prefer either the Cabernets or the more full-bodied red Zinfandels.

If you are looking for festive alcoholic alternatives to beer and wine you may want to consider serving the following summer drinks that can accommodate large parties either because all the preparation time is completed before your guests arrive or the time required to mix a large amount after your guests have arrived is very short.

Frozen Daiquiri

My mother has served this drink for years to both adults and children. The children receive the nonalcoholic version but they feel like adults; the look is similar and they receive their drinks in the same style cups as the adults.

This is a refreshing summer drink that will easily quench thirsts and is best served with the appetizer while your guests are eagerly awaiting the entree.

Rum Based Daiquiri

In a large container mix the following together: **1 liter bottle of lemon-lime soda, one large can (12 ounces) of frozen lemonade** that has been thawed, **2 lemonade cans of water**, and **1 lemonade can of light rum**. The above 4 ingredients will add up to a total of 2-1/2 quarts of liquid. Stir well and transfer to a large plastic container and place in the freezer until frozen (at least 6 hours).

Once your guests have arrived, remove from the freezer and spoon a portion of the contents into a blender. Blend until smooth and pour into small glasses. Serve immediately.

The alcoholic strength can be adjusted by increasing or decreasing the amount of water and correspondingly decreasing or increasing the amount of rum.

Alcohol-Free Daiquiri

Repeat the above steps except eliminate the rum and use 3 cans of water instead of 2. Also, you may want to use **pink lemonade** instead of regular lemonade so you will be able to tell which glasses contain the rum.

Servings: 8 to 12

Frozen Banana Daiquiri

This recipe is similar to the previous recipe for Frozen Daiquiris except that it has a wonderful fruity taste and need not be prepared ahead of time. Six hours before your guests arrive, you can prepare the first alternative, Frozen Daiquiris, and, when your guests arrive, prepare this one and offer them the choice of a frozen daiquiri, with or without fruit.

To a blender add the following ingredients: **4 cups of ice cubes, 3/4 cup of lime juice, 1/3 cup of Triple Sec, 3/4 cup of light rum, 1 tablespoon of sugar, and 3 medium-size ripe bananas**. Blend well until the ingredients turn to a slurry. Serve immediately.

The alcoholic strength can be adjusted by increasing or decreasing the amount of ice or the amount of rum.

Servings: 4

Frozen Strawberry Daiquiri

This recipe is similar to the previous recipe for Frozen Banana Daiquiris except that the nonalcoholic version tastes just as wonderful as its traditional rum based cousin. When your guests arrive, offer them the choice of a frozen fruit daiquiri, with or without rum. My children look forward to this alcohol-free fruit drink not only because of its great taste but also because it is a nice diversion from canned and bottled soda.

Rum-Based Daiquiri

To a blender add the following ingredients: **3/4 cup of lime juice, 3/4 cup of light rum, 1 tablespoon of sugar, 2 cups of sliced fresh strawberries**, and slowly blend in **ice cubes** (approximately 4 cups) until the mixture turns to a slurry. Serve immediately.

Alcohol-Free Daiquiri

Repeat the above steps except eliminate the rum and use **1/2 of a cup of orange juice** instead of 3/4 of a cup of light rum.

Servings: 4

Frozen Planter's Punch

This recipe resembles the Frozen Daiquiri (see page 140) recipe except that it is less tart. While it can be served over ice, I think that it tastes better if blended with the ice until smooth.

Mix in a blender the following ingredients: **4 cups of ice, 1/4 cup of Rose's Lime Juice, 1/8 cup of lemon juice, 1/8 cup of orange juice, 1 tablespoon of Triple Sec**, and **3/4 cup of rum.** Blend well until the ingredients turn to a slurry. Serve immediately.

The alcoholic strength can be adjusted by increasing or decreasing the amount of ice or rum that is added.

Servings: 4

Frozen Margarita

Excluding beer and wine, this is one of the easiest and least troublesome alcoholic drinks to prepare for large groups.

Add the following ingredients to a blender: **4 cups of ice, 1/4 cup of Rose's Lime Juice, 1/4 cup of lime juice, 1/3 cup of Triple Sec**, and **1/2 cup of tequila.** Blend well until the ingredients turn to a slurry. Serve immediately.

The alcoholic strength can be adjusted by increasing or decreasing the amount of ice or tequila.

Servings: 4

Banana Foster

This beverage is intended to be served either as the only dessert or as an accompaniment to a dessert such as Grilled Pound Cake (see page 135). This beverage is very soothing after a grilled meal, especially a spicy grilled meal.

Add the following to the blender: **8 scoops of vanilla ice cream, 3/4 cup of rum, 1/4 cup of Triple Sec,** and **4 medium-size ripe bananas.** Blend well until the ingredients turn to a slurry. Serve immediately.

The alcoholic strength can be adjusted by increasing or decreasing the amount of rum.

Servings: 4

Red or White Wine Sangria

This is another great summer drink that compliments any grilled meal and adds more festive touches to your get-together, whether large or small.

In a large pitcher or pot dissolve **1/4 cup of granulated sugar** in **1 cup of water**. Add **1 bottle (750 ml) of red or white wine (preferably Spanish wine** in keeping with the theme), **1 thinly sliced orange,** and **1 thinly sliced lime** (as an option, add **1 red apple** that has been cut into small wedges). Refrigerate for 1 hour or more.

Pour sangria into wine glasses containing ice. Add slices of fruit to each glass. Serve immediately.

Servings: 8 to 10 per bottle of wine

Spritzer or Wine Cooler

During the hot summer months a wine spritzer (white wine) or a wine cooler (red wine) can serve as a refreshing light beverage since the wine is diluted with club soda. Served over ice, these "light" wine drinks can cool the intensity of the spiciest of grilled meals.

Add **4 ice cubes** to a wine glass and **1/3 cup of red or white wine.** Fill the remaining glass with **club soda.** Serve immediately.

The alcoholic strength can be adjusted by increasing or decreasing the amount of wine.

Servings: 8 to 10 per bottle of wine

Top Fifteen Favorite Grilled Meals

As promised earlier, this chapter contains my list of favorite grilled meals. The meals are ordered beginning with the kick-off to the summer season—Memorial Day weekend, and continue through the year ending with Mother's Day. Each meal is complete with appetizer, entree, vegetable/side dish, and beverage, but excludes dessert (I will leave that to your imagination). Just about every holiday or special occasion can be celebrated with one of these meals.

In addition to the list of courses for each meal, a simple-to-follow timeline describing when to perform each activity for the selected meal is also included. The timeline is constructed to place each grilling activity as close as possible to MGT (Minimalist Grill Time) + 0, the moment when the charcoal is ready for grilling. The timeline is arranged so you enjoy the appetizer well ahead of the entree and that the entree and vegetables/side dishes are ready simultaneously. You may begin certain activities, like marinating the meat, a day ahead of the party and not just several hours before placing it on the grill. Also, you may wait as long as you wish to grill the food—not just as soon as the charcoal is ready.

Have fun with these meal selections and don't hesitate to experiment with your own combinations.

Meal One:
Summer Kick-Off Meal

Appetizer
Grilled Quesadilla
Entree
Grilled Basic Hamburgers and Grilled Hot Dogs
Veg./Side Dish
Cole Slaw and Slightly Spicy Baked Beans
Beverage
Frozen Daiquiri

Time Chart

MGT - 6 hours	Prepare alcoholic (adult) and non-alcoholic (child) daiquiris and place in freezer
MGT - 4 hours	Prepare cole slaw
MGT - 25 min.	Light charcoal
MGT - 20	Prepare quesadillas
MGT + 0	Spread coals
MGT + 5	Add quesadillas to grill
MGT + 15	Remove quesadillas from grill and serve
MGT + 25	Prepare baked beans
MGT + 35	Place hamburgers on grill
MGT + 40	Add hot dogs to grill
MGT + 50	Remove hamburgers and hot dogs from grill, and serve with cole slaw and baked beans

(serve daiquiris with appetizer and entree)

Meal Two:
Father's Day Meal

Appetizer
Grilled Bruschetta
Entree
Grilled Pork Tenderloin
Veg./Side Dish
Grilled Corn and Cole Slaw
Beverage
Red Wine Sangria

Time Chart

MGT - 7 hours	Marinate pork
MGT - 4 hours	Prepare cole slaw
MGT - 1 hour	Prepare sangria
MGT - 1 hour	Prepare topping for bruschetta
MGT - 30 min.	Prepare garlic oil for bruschetta
MGT - 25	Light charcoal
MGT - 20	Wrap corn in foil
MGT + 0	Spread coals
MGT + 5	Add bread for bruschetta to grill
MGT + 10	Remove bread from grill and serve with topping
MGT + 20	Place corn on grill
MGT + 20	Add pork tenderloin to grill
MGT + 40	Remove corn from grill but do not unwrap
MGT + 45	Remove pork tenderloin from grill, unwrap corn, and serve with cole slaw

(serve sangria with appetizer and entree)

Meal Three:
Catch-of-the-Day Meal

Appetizer
Gazpacho Soup
Entree
Medley of Shrimp (Grilled and Marinated)
Grilled Salmon, Grilled Tuna, and Grilled Swordfish
Veg./Side Dish
Grilled String Beans and Favorite Rice
Beverage
White Wine Sangria

Time Chart

MGT - 7 hours	Prepare marinade for Marinated Shrimp and add 1/2 of shrimp to marinade
MGT - 3 hours	Prepare soup
MGT - 1 hour	Prepare sangria
MGT - 45 min.	Prepare black bean and lime salsa
MGT - 25	Light charcoal
MGT - 10	Parboil string beans
MGT - 5	Start rice cooking*
MGT + 0	Spread coals
MGT + 5	Serve soup
MGT + 5	Add string beans to grill
MGT + 10	Add swordfish to grill
MGT + 15	Add all remaining fish to grill
MGT + 25	Remove fish and string beans from grill and serve with rice

(serve sangria with appetizer and entree)

*Assumes 30 minute rice

Meal Four:

Fourth of July Meal

Appetizer

Summer Salsa and Chips

Entree

Pulled Beef Sandwiches and Grilled Hot Dogs

Veg./Side Dish

Cole Slaw and Slightly Spicy Baked Beans

Beverage

Beer and Soda

Time Chart

MGT - ?	Arrange weeks or several days before party to have guests bring an appetizer, salad, or a dessert to share
MGT - 4 hours	Prepare cole slaw
MGT - 2 hours	Prepare salsa
MGT - 1 hour	Chill beer and soda
MGT - 25 min.	Light charcoal
MGT + 0	Spread coals
MGT + 5	Add beef to grill
MGT + 45	Add charcoal to coals
MGT + 90	Add charcoal to coals
MGT + 90	Prepare sauce for beef sandwiches
MGT + 90	Remove beef from grill and let sit
MGT + 135	Add charcoal to coals
MGT + 150	Shred beef (takes 30 minutes)
MGT + 155	Prepare baked beans
MGT + 170	Add hot dogs to grill
MGT + 180	Remove hot dogs from grill, add beef to sauce and place on buns, and serve with cole slaw, and baked beans

(serve the summer salsa and chips before the entree)

Meal Five:

Informal Children's Meal

Appetizer
Grilled Nachos
Entree
Wood-Smoked Pizza with Favorite Toppings
Veg./Side dish
Boston lettuce with Vinaigrette Dressing
Beverage
Soda

Time Chart

MGT - 2 hours	Prepare pizza dough
MGT - 1 hour	Chill soda
MGT - 30 min.	Spread dough to form pizza shell (with help from children)
MGT - 30	Soak wood chips
MGT - 30	Mix vinaigrette dressing
MGT - 25	Light charcoal
MGT + 0	Spread coals
MGT + 5	Add nachos to grill
MGT + 15	Remove nachos and serve
MGT + 20	Serve salad with dressing
MGT + 30	Add wood chips to coals and place raw pizza dough on grill
MGT + 35	Remove pizza dough from grill and add sauce, cheese, and toppings (with help from children)
MGT + 45	Return pizza to grill
MGT + 55	Remove pizza from grill and serve

Meal Six:
Universally-Liked by All Meal

Appetizer
Grilled Quesadilla
Entree
Barbecue-Sauced Chicken Tenders
Veg./Side Dish
Grilled String Beans and Grilled Potato Chips
Beverage
Frozen Daiquiri

Time Chart

MGT - 6 hours	Prepare alcoholic (adult) and nonalcoholic (child) daiquiris
MGT - 1 hour	Prepare barbecue sauce (unless using store-bought sauce)
MGT - 25 min.	Light charcoal
MGT - 20	Prepare quesadillas and potato chips
MGT - 10	Parboil string beans
MGT + 0	Spread coals
MGT + 5	Add quesadillas to grill
MGT + 15	Remove quesadillas from grill and serve
MGT + 20	Add potato chips and string beans to grill
MGT + 25	Add chicken to grill
MGT + 40	Remove chicken, potato chips and string beans from grill and serve

(Serve daiquiris with appetizer and entree)

Meal Seven:

Festive Party Meal

Appetizer
Grilled Shrimp Cocktail
Entree
Grilled Steak Fajitas
Veg./Side Dish
Slightly Spicy Baked Beans and Spanish Rice
Beverage
Margaritas

Time Chart

MGT - 5 hours	Add steak to marinade
MGT - 25 min.	Light charcoal
MGT - 10	Prepare margaritas
MGT + 0	Spread coals
MGT + 5	Add shrimp to grill
MGT + 15	Remove shrimp from grill and serve
MGT + 15	Start rice cooking*
MGT + 20	Prepare baked beans
MGT + 25	Add steak to grill
MGT + 35	Add tortillas to grill to warm
MGT + 45	Remove steak and tortillas from grill and serve with accompaniments, baked beans, and rice

(Serve margaritas with appetizer and entree)

*Assumes 30 minute rice

Meal Eight:
No Special Occasion Meal

Appetizer
Grilled Polenta
Entree
Herb-Smoked Pork Chops
Veg./Side Dish
Grilled Asparagus and Slightly Spicy Baked Beans
Beverage
Beer

Time Chart

MGT - 4 hours	Prepare polenta
MGT - 1 hour	Chill beer
MGT - 25 min.	Light charcoal
MGT + 0	Spread coals
MGT + 5	Place sliced polenta on grill
MGT + 15	Prepare baked beans
MGT + 20	Remove polenta from grill and serve
MGT + 20	Add pork chops and sage to grill
MGT + 30	Add asparagus to grill
MGT + 40	Remove pork chops and asparagus from grill and serve with baked beans

Meal Nine:
Elegant Dinner Meal

Appetizer
Grilled Bruschetta
Entree
Grilled Swordfish
Veg./Side Dish
Grilled Broccoli and Favorite Rice
Beverage
White Wine

Time Chart

MGT - 2 hours	Chill white wine
MGT - 60 min.	Prepare topping for bruschetta
MGT - 60	Prepare garlic oil for bruschetta
MGT - 30	Prepare black bean and lime salsa
MGT - 25	Light charcoal
MGT - 10	Parboil broccoli
MGT + 0	Spread coals
MGT + 5	Start rice cooking*
MGT + 10	Place bread for bruschetta on grill
MGT + 15	Remove bread from grill and serve with topping
MGT + 20	Add swordfish to grill
MGT + 20	Add broccoli to grill
MGT + 35	Remove swordfish and broccoli from grill and serve with rice

(serve wine with appetizer and entree)

*Assumes 30 minute rice

Meal Ten:
End-of-Summer Meal

Appetizer
Grilled Bruschetta
Entree
Barbecue-Sauced Pork Ribs
Veg./Side Dish
Slightly Spicy Baked Beans and Cole Slaw
Beverage
Red Wine Sangria

Time Chart

MGT - 4 hours	Prepare cole slaw
MGT - 1 hour	Prepare sangria
MGT - 1 hour	Prepare topping for bruschetta
MGT - 40 min.	Prepare garlic oil for bruschetta
MGT - 30	Prepare sauce for ribs
MGT - 25	Light charcoal
MGT + 0	Spread coals
MGT + 5	Add bread for bruschetta to grill
MGT + 10	Remove bread from grill and serve with topping
MGT + 15	Add ribs to grill
MGT + 25	Prepare baked beans
MGT + 50	Remove ribs from grill and serve with baked beans and cole slaw

(Serve sangria with appetizer and entree)

Meal Eleven:
Hearty Man's Meal

Appetizer
Tomatoes with Mozzarella and Onions
Entree
Grilled Filet Mignon or Sirloin Steak
Veg./Side Dish
Grilled Onions and Grilled Potato Chips
Beverage
Red Wine (Cabernet or Zinfandel)

Time Chart

MGT - 25 min.	Light charcoal
MGT - 20	Prepare potato chips
MGT + 0	Spread coals
MGT + 5	Slice tomatoes, onions, and cheese and serve
MGT + 20	Add potato chips to grill
MGT + 25	Add steak and onions to grill
MGT + 35	Remove steak, onions, and potato chips from grill and serve

(Serve wine with appetizer and entree)

Meal Twelve: Thanksgiving Day (Christmas Eve or Day) Meal

Appetizer
None
Entree
Smoked Turkey
Veg./Side Dish
String Beans or Peas, Stuffing, Potatoes, and Cranberries
Beverage
Red wine (Zinfandel)

Time Chart

MGT - 30 min.	Soak wood chips
MGT - 25	Light charcoal
MGT + 0	Spread coals, add wood chips, and place turkey on grill
MGT + 30	Add wood chips to coals
MGT + 45	Add charcoal to coals
MGT + 60	Add wood chips to coals
MGT + 90	Add wood chips and charcoal to coals
MGT + 120	Add wood chips to coals
MGT + 135	Add charcoal to coals
MGT + 150	Add wood chips to coals
MGT + 165	Add stuffing to grill
MGT + 180	Remove turkey from grill (internal temperature should be 175-180 degrees) and let rest before carving
MGT + 195	Remove stuffing from grill
MGT + 200	Carve turkey and serve with vegetables, dressing, and other side dishes

(Note: stuffing should be prepared and ready for grilling at MGT + 165 min. Vegetables and side dishes should be ready by MGT + 200 min. Serve wine with main entree.)

Meal Thirteen:
Valentine's Day Meal

Appetizer
Grilled Portobello Mushrooms
Entree
Smoked Salmon
Veg./Side Dish
Grilled String Beans and Favorite Rice
Beverage
Chilled Champagne

Time Chart

MGT - 2 hours	Chill champagne
MGT - 30 min.	Soak wood chips
MGT - 25	Light charcoal
MGT - 10	Parboil string beans
MGT + 0	Spread coals and place mushrooms on grill
MGT + 15	Remove mushrooms from grill and serve
MGT + 15	Add wood chips to coals
MGT + 15	Add salmon to grill
MGT + 45	Add wood chips and charcoal to coals
MGT + 50	Start rice cooking*
MGT + 60	Add string beans to grill
MGT + 80	Remove salmon and string beans from grill and serve with rice

(Serve champagne with appetizer and entree)

*Assumes 30 minute rice

Meal Fourteen:

Easter Sunday Meal

Appetizer
Smoked Trout
Entree
Grilled Leg of Lamb
Veg./Side Dish
Grilled Asparagus and Favorite Rice
Beverage
White Wine and Red Wine (Cabernet)

Time Chart

MGT - 7 hours	Marinate lamb and add trout to salt water bath
MGT - 2 hours	Chill white wine
MGT - 30 min.	Soak wood chips
MGT - 25	Light charcoal
MGT + 0	Spread coals, add wood chips, and place trout on grill
MGT + 35	Remove trout from grill and serve
MGT + 45	Add charcoal to coals
MGT + 45	Add lamb to grill
MGT + 55	Start rice cooking*
MGT + 75	Add asparagus to grill
MGT + 80	Remove lamb from grill and let sit at room temperature
MGT + 85	Serve lamb with asparagus and rice

(Serve white wine with appetizer and red wine with entree)

*Assumes 30 minute rice

Meal Fifteen:
Mother's Day Meal

Appetizer
Grilled Crab Cakes
Entree
Grilled Marinated Chicken
Veg./Side Dish
Grilled Broccoli and Favorite Rice
Beverage
White Wine

Time Chart

MGT - 3 hours	Add chicken to marinade
MGT - 2 hours	Chill white wine
MGT - 25 min.	Light charcoal
MGT - 10	Parboil broccoli
MGT + 0	Spread coals
MGT + 5	Add crab cakes to grill
MGT + 10	Start rice cooking*
MGT + 20	Remove crab cakes and serve
MGT + 25	Add chicken to grill
MGT + 25	Add broccoli to grill
MGT + 40	Remove chicken and broccoli from grill and serve with rice

(serve wine with appetizer and entree)

*Assumes 30 minute rice

Afterword

I hope that you enjoy using my grilling and smoking techniques to prepare many of the enclosed recipes.

I have provided the best of my minimalist recipes, which include dishes from my family and friends as well as those that I have perfected over the years. I don't think you will need any more than these; in fact, there are probably very few remaining recipes true to the minimalist theme that could be added to this handbook. The number of recipes in the handbook is enough to provide even the most avid griller several year's worth of variety. Of course, I encourage you to experiment with your own variations on any recipe. But remember—elegance in simplicity. Prime meat, fish, and vegetables taste best with minimal ingredients, assuming you have the right equipment and employ the proper grilling techniques.

I hope in a not-too-distant time you will become your neighborhood's newest Minimalist Griller!

Basic Measurements Table

3 teaspoons = 1 tablespoon
4 tablespoons = 1/4 cup
5-1/3 tablespoons = 1/3 cup
16 tablespoons = 1 cup
1 cup = 8 ounces = 1/2 pint
2 cups = 16 ounces = 1 pint
4 cups = 32 ounces = 2 pints = 1 quart
2 teaspoons of minced garlic = 3 minced garlic cloves
1/2 cup of chopped onion = 1 medium-size chopped onion

Index